Shadowlands

by William Nicholson

SAMUEL FRENCH, INC.
45 WEST 25TH STREET   NEW YORK 10010
7623 SUNSET BOULEVARD HOLLYWOOD 90046
LONDON   TORONTO

ISBN 0 573 69313 7   Printed in U.S.A.   #21105

IMPORTANT BILLING AND CREDIT REQUIREMENTS

Shadowlands was originally presented at The Theatre Royal, Plymouth, on 5th October, 1989, the play was first presented in London at the Queen's Theatre, on 23rd October, 1989, by Brian Eastman and Armada Productions in association with The Theatre Royal, Plymouth, by arrangement with Stoll Moss Theatres Ltd. The cast was as follows:

C. S. Lewis .... Nigel Hawthorne
Major W. H. Lewis ("Warnie")... Geoffrey Toone
Professor Christopher Riley........ Philip Anthony
Rev. "Harry" Harrington .... Allan Mitchell
Alan Gregg/Doctor .... Christopher Brown
Dr. Maurice Oakley/Waiter in Tea
Room/Priest .... Geoffrey Drew
Joy Gresham, née Davidman........ Jane Lapotaire
Douglas .... Ilan Ostrove or
                               James Holland
Registrar/ Nurse .... Sheila Ferris
Registrar's Clerk/Waiter in Hotel......Ray Daniels

Directed by Elijah Moshinsky
Designed by Mark Thompson

Shadowlands opened on November 11, 1990, at the Brooks Atkinson Theatre in New York City, with the following cast:

C. S. Lewis .... Nigel Hawthorne
Christopher Riley........................ Paul Sparer
Rev. "Harry" Harrington .... Robin Chadwick
Dr. Oakley............................. Hugh A. Rose
Alan Gregg .... Edmund C. Davys
Major W. H. Lewis ("Warnie")... Michael Allinson
Douglas .... Jonathan Gold, Lance Robinson
Joy Davidman....................... Jane Alexander
Waiter .... Hugh A. Rose
Registrar .... Mary Layne
Clerk .... Hugh A. Rose
Nurse.................................. Mary Layne
Doctor............................ Edmund C. Davys
Priest .... Hugh A. Rose

Director .... Elijah Moshinsky
Sets and Costume Designer ...... Mark Thompson
Lighting Designer.............. John Michael Deegan
Casting.............................. Marjorie Martin
General Manager.................... Ralph Roseman
Production Stage Manager........ Elliott Woodruff

CHARACTERS

C. S. LEWIS, an Oxford don in his fifties; known as "Jack"

JOY GRESHAM, an American in her late thirties

MAJOR WARNIE LEWIS, Lewis's bachelor brother

CHRISTOPHER RILEY, an Oxford don

HARRY HARRINGTON, an Oxford chaplain

DOUGLAS, Joy's eight-year-old son

ALAN GREGG/DOCTOR

REGISTRAR/NURSE

PRIEST/WAITER/

DR. MAURICE OAKLEY/CLERK

The action takes place in Oxford in the 1950s.

ACT I

The stage is divided into two areas, one within the other. The inner area, which takes up most of the stage, is concealed by a translucent screen.

LEWIS enters, holding a newspaper, and, standing before the screen, addresses the audience as if they have come to hear one of his popular talks.

LEWIS. Good evening. The subject of my talk tonight is love, pain, and suffering.

Of course, as a comfortably situated middle-aged bachelor, I must be quite an authority on pain and love, wouldn't you have thought?

Now, by "pain" I don't mean a nagging discomfort in the intestines. For that matter, by "love" I don't mean a nagging discomfort in the intestines, either. The question I will put to you this evening, and one which I will attempt to answer, is this: If God loves us, why does He allow us to suffer so much? War. Pestilence. Famine.

(HE waves his newspaper at the audience.)

LEWIS. This is this morning's paper. Last night, as I'm sure you know, a number 1 bus drove into a column of young Royal Marine cadets in Chatham, and killed twenty-three of them. They were ten-year-old boys, marching and singing on their way to a boxing match. The road was

7

unlit. The driver didn't see them. It was a terrible accident. Nobody was to blame. Except ...

(HE points an accusing finger upwards.)

LEWIS. Now, where was He? Why didn't He stop it? What possible point can there be to such a tragedy? Isn't God supposed to be good? Isn't God supposed to love us?

Now, that's the nub of the matter: love. I think I'm right in saying that by "love," most of us mean either kindness or being "in love." But surely when we say that God loves us we don't mean that God is in love with us ... do we? Not sitting by the telephone, writing letters: "I love you madly—God, xxx and hugs." At least I don't think so. Perhaps we mean that He's a kind God. Kindness is the desire to see others happy. Not happy in this way or that, but just happy.

Perhaps we mean that He loves us with a more mature benevolence. Not so much a Father in heaven as a Grandfather. "I do like to see the young people enjoying themselves ... What does it matter as long as it makes them happy?"

Here I'm going to say something which may come as a bit of a shock. I think that God doesn't necessarily want us to be happy. He wants us to be lovable. Worthy of love. Able to be loved by Him. We don't start off being all that lovable, if we're honest. What makes people hard to love? Isn't it what is commonly called selfishness? Selfish people are hard to love because so little love comes out of them.

God creates us free, free to be selfish, but He adds a mechanism that will penetrate our selfishness and wake us up to the presence of others in the world, and that mechanism is called suffering. To put it in another way, pain is God's megaphone to rouse a deaf world. Why must it be pain? Why can't He wake us more gently, with violins or laughter? Because the dream from which we must be awakened is the dream that all is well.

Now that is the most dangerous illusion of them all. Self-sufficiency is the enemy of salvation. If you are self-sufficient, you have no need of God. If you have no need of God, you do not seek Him. If you do not seek Him, you will not find Him.

God loves us, so He makes us the gift of suffering. Through suffering, we release our hold on the toys of this world, and know our true good lies in another world.

We're like blocks of stone, out of which the sculptor carves the forms of men. The blows of His chisel, which hurt us so much, are what make us perfect. The suffering in the world is not the failure of God's love for us; it is that love in action.

For believe me, this world that seems to us so substantial is no more than the shadowlands. Real life has not begun yet.

(As LEWIS exits, the screen rises to reveal the magnificently furnished high table of an Oxford college dining hall. This is the traditional all-male world to which Lewis belongs.

Round the table sit CHRISTOPHER RILEY, HARRY HARRINGTON, MAURICE OAKLEY, ALAN GREGG, and MAJOR WARNIE LEWIS. WARNIE is drinking more than is good for him.

A ripple of LAUGHTER rises from the table. RILEY is holding forth.)

OAKLEY. Then she said, "Oh yes, I know, the unspeakable in pursuit of the inedible."

RILEY. I said to the lady on my left that animals are merciless killers, and regularly eat one another alive. We had a short, and I thought productive, exchange about the moral superiority of herbivores to carnivores, at the end of which I suggested the logic of her position was that she should execute her cats. She then said, "Why are you trying to upset me? You don't even know me."

(LEWIS enters and takes his place at the table during this speech.

GREGG, to whom Riley's argument has chiefly been addressed, responds with common-man vigor.)

GREGG. So? What's that supposed to prove?

LEWIS. I think Christopher means us to conclude that women are different.

RILEY. Thank you, Jack. Women are different.

GREGG. It seems to me the poor woman was clearly terrified.

LEWIS. I like her saying, "Why are you upsetting me? You don't even know me." She's right, of course. One does only seek to distress one's friends.

GREGG. Different in what way, exactly?

RILEY. The point is this, Alan. She was unable to distinguish between an intellectual attack and an emotional attack.

HARRINGTON. Even so, Christopher, some women are very clever, you know.

OAKLEY. Jack, you don't hold with this, do you? You're a great respecter of women.

RILEY. Hah! It's all that depth of personal experience.

LEWIS. Christopher believes only practicing fornicators can teach him sexual morality. Or do you believe each man must fornicate for himself? I've never been quite clear.

RILEY. In a sense, perhaps I do. Morality presupposes choices. The man who has never fornicated, or wanted to fornicate, or imagined fornicating, has no real moral choice in the matter. To fornicate or not to fornicate, that is the question.

LEWIS. Ah, Christopher. Beware solipsism. Soon you'll be believing if it hasn't happened to you, it doesn't exist.

RILEY. I'm sure you're right, Jack. Already I believe if it hasn't happened to me, it doesn't matter.

HARRINGTON. Come along now, Jack. We're relying on you to speak up for the weaker sex.

RILEY. Yes, Jack, why not? You're a writer of fantasies.

LEWIS. I do talk to women, Christopher.

RILEY. Really?

LEWIS. Really.

RILEY. Name one woman you've spoken to this week.

LEWIS. I addressed a conference of women on Monday, as it happens.

RILEY. Ah, but did they address you?

LEWIS. I get letters. Women write me letters.

RILEY. Do you write back?

LEWIS. Yes, of course.

RILEY. Pen pals. Well, well. Epistolary intimacies. *Liaisons dangereuses.*

LEWIS. I don't profess any special insights on the subjects. Harry here's the married man.

HARRINGTON. Speaking of which …

LEWIS. Yes, off you go.

GREGG. I must be off too.

(This leads to a general move to leave the table. HARRINGTON and GREGG exit.

RILEY is on the point of leaving when WARNIE, a little drunk, rises and starts to recite.)

WARNIE.

'Twas an evening in November,

As I very well remember

I was walking down the street in drunken pride,

My knees were all aflutter

So I lay down in the gutter,

And a pig came up and lay down by my side.

As I lay there in the gutter

Thinking thoughts I could not utter,

A lady passing by was heard to say.

"You can tell a man who boozes,

By the company he chooses."

And the pig got up and slowly walked away.

(RILEY and LEWIS exchange a glance.)

RILEY. Good night, Lewis Major. Good night, Lewis Minor.

LEWIS. Good night, Christopher.

(RILEY exits.
LEWIS knows WARNIE is drunk, and is discreetly
protective of him.)

LEWIS. You and your pig. Come on, big brother.

(BOTH leave the inner set. The screen falls. THEY put on
hats and scarves and stroll slowly home in front of the
screen.)

WARNIE. Thanks for the dinner, Jack.

LEWIS. Decent claret, I thought.

WARNIE. Very decent.

LEWIS. Shall we treat ourselves to a cab?

WARNIE. Oh no. I think I'm up to a toddle.

LEWIS. Whatever you say, Warnie.

GREGG. *(Passes by on his bicycle, heading home.)*
Good night.

(THEY wish him good night.)

WARNIE. That young Gregg—hasn't quite got it, has
he?

LEWIS. He's all right. Give him time.

WARNIE. Young people are so serious. Though no
more than us, I daresay. Matter of style.

LEWIS. Christopher used to be quite serious. I
remember him getting quite heated about the abdication.

WARNIE. Thought the king was unfairly treated, did
he?

LEWIS. No, no. He thought he ought to be guillotined.

WARNIE. Tell you something I've noticed, Jack. Christopher lives the life of a monk, and talks about nothing but women. Harry's married, and never says a word about his wife.

LEWIS. What shall we conclude from that, Warnie? That women are more interesting in theory than in practice?

WARNIE. I find it safer never to conclude anything.

LEWIS. (*Stands gazing up at the night sky.*) Going to be a frost tonight.

WARNIE. Too many stars. Confuses me.

LEWIS. Oh, Warnie. You're as bad as Christopher.

WARNIE. Good dinner. Always is. Good night, Jack.

LEWIS. Good night, Warnie.

(*WARNIE exits. The screen rises to reveal the study at The Kilns, Lewis's home. LEWIS enters and pulls a dressing gown on over his jacket.*)

LEWIS.
> Here he lies where he longed to be,
> Home is the sailor, home from sea,
> And the hunter home from the hill.

(*The set is dominated by a giant wardrobe at the back. It is the size a normal wardrobe would appear to a small child.*
LEWIS goes to his desk and settles down to writing letters. For a few moments there is silence.
The LIGHTS change to indicate that it is now morning.

*WARNIE enters, carrying a tray of breakfast, the morning
    paper, and the morning post. In what is clearly a
    familiar procedure, HE pauses as HE passes Lewis at
    his desk, and LEWIS reaches up and takes the letters
    from the tray. WARNIE then sets down the tray and
    pours them both coffee, while LEWIS flicks through
    the letters. HE selects an airmail letter to read first.*
*Their conversation now has the appearance of dialogue, but
    really it is two intersecting monologues; the fruit of the
    long years they have lived together.)*

WARNIE. I had the strangest dream last night.

LEWIS. Another dispatch from Mrs. Gresham.

WARNIE. Can't remember any of it.

LEWIS. The Jewish Communist Christian American.

WARNIE. You may ask me how I know it was strange
if I've forgotten it. Can't answer that one.

(HE settles down with his paper. LEWIS reads his letter.)

LEWIS. She's very persistent. "Which would you rather
be, Mr. Lewis? The child caught in the magic spell, or the
magician casting it?"

WARNIE. No news, of course. Never is any.

LEWIS. I find that I'm quite curious about her.

WARNIE. About who?

LEWIS. Mrs. Gresham.

WARNIE. Why's that?

LEWIS. Her letters are unusual. She writes as if she
knows me.

WARNIE. How can she?

LEWIS. I don't know. I suppose she's read my books.

WARNIE. I expect it's just the American style. Americans don't understand about inhibitions.

LEWIS. She's called Joy.

WARNIE. One can't hold her responsible for that.

(LEWIS comes upon a surprising section in the letter. HE takes it and shows it to Warnie.)

LEWIS. Look at that, Warnie. Top line.

WARNIE. She's coming to England.

LEWIS. Yes.

WARNIE. "I'm told you share a house with your brother, Major Lewis." Who can have told her that?

LEWIS. You remember that American who came and wrote a sort of book about me? She knows him.

WARNIE. Ah. "I imagine you telling your brother about me, and him saying, 'Is she a nut?,' and you weighing this letter in one hand as if to weigh my respectability, and saying, 'I'm not sure.' " *(HE gives the letter back.)* Is she a nut?

LEWIS. *(Smiles and weighs the letter in his hand.)* I'm not sure.

WARNIE. She seems to want to meet you.

LEWIS. Us.

WARNIE. Politeness.

LEWIS. A good sign.

WARNIE. You are curious.

LEWIS. When you correspond with someone, you do begin to form an impression. You wonder whether the impression is correct. Now, what do you say, Warnie? I see her as rather short and dumpy.

WARNIE. Spectacles.

LEWIS. Certainly not a beauty.

WARNIE. Long, pointed nose.

LEWIS. Leopard-skin coat and red hat. Brown eyes.

WARNIE. Beady.

LEWIS. No, I don't think so. More ... probing.

WARNIE. Pushy.

LEWIS. She suggests tea, in a hotel. That shows some delicacy, I think.

WARNIE. Tea is safe. A hotel is safe.

LEWIS. Shall we say yes?

WARNIE. She might be mad. Remember the one who put an announcement in the papers saying you'd married her?

LEWIS. Oh, I don't think so. Though she does write poems.

WARNIE. Then she is bonkers.

LEWIS. It is possible.

WARNIE. I suppose if she's coming all the way from New York to see you ...

LEWIS. Good heavens, Warnie, what gives you that idea? No, I'm just a day excursion. Blenheim Palace. Wookey Hole. Tea with the Lewis brothers.

WARNIE. With you.

LEWIS. I'm not going alone.

WARNIE. Well. If you want to, Jack.

(THEY leave the inner set. The screen falls. The downstage area becomes the tea room of an Oxford hotel.
WARNIE and LEWIS look around with some uncertainty.)

WARNIE. How will we know which one is her?

LEWIS. I suppose her little boy will be with her.

WARNIE. What if there are two middle-aged ladies with small boys?

LEWIS. We must hope they don't all want to have tea with us.

(A WOMAN enters, crossing the stage.)

LEWIS. Now, there's a woman. Good afternoon.

WOMAN. Good afternoon. *(SHE exits.)*

LEWIS. You see, no little boy.

WARNIE. What's the boy's name?

LEWIS. Douglas.

WARNIE. You won't be *too* agreeable, will you, Jack?

LEWIS. Don't worry, Warnie. We'll put her back on the 4:57 to Paddington.

WARNIE. She'll turn out to be writing a dissertation on your works. She'll ask if she can come and watch you while you create. She'll say, "I'll sit in a corner and you'll never know I'm there." She'll ask you how you get your ideas. She'll take flash photographs.

LEWIS. It's only tea. An hour or so of polite conversation. Then we go home, and everything goes on just the way it always has.

(An eight-year-old BOY enters and looks around. HE carries a book. This is DOUGLAS.

A sensible-looking WOMAN follows the boy and looks around the room. SHE looks neither mad nor obviously American. In fact, she is rather attractive. This is JOY.)

LEWIS. It's her, Warnie.

WARNIE. Surely not?

LEWIS. I think so.

(JOY sees them and crosses the room to them. THEY rise. SHE holds out her hand.)

JOY. Mr. Lewis?
LEWIS. Mrs. Gresham?
JOY. I'm Joy Gresham.
LEWIS. How do you do? This is my brother, Major Lewis.
JOY. Major Lewis. And this is Douglas.

(DOUGLAS is standing staring at Lewis.)

LEWIS. Hello, Douglas.
DOUGLAS. Is that him?
JOY. That's him.
DOUGLAS. It doesn't look like him.

(This produces a general LAUGH.)

LEWIS. I'm sorry, Douglas. Yours is, I'm afraid, a common reaction. Please sit down, Mrs. Gresham, and we'll summon up some tea. Warnie, would you mind ringing the old whatsis. That is, if you drink tea.
JOY. Of course. This is England.
LEWIS. So it is.

(WARNIE has rung the bell for the WAITER, who appears.)

WARNIE. Tea for three, please.

LEWIS. I get the feeling you share Douglas's opinion. I don't look like him.

JOY. Oh, I'm sorry. It's just that I've imagined this moment.

LEWIS. And it's not as you imagined?

JOY. Not exactly. It's kind of you to find time to meet me. So many people must write you. You can't be forever having tea with strange women.

LEWIS. Not completely strange, Mrs. Gresham. I've enjoyed our correspondence.

JOY. Enjoyed? Okay.

LEWIS. Not the word you would use?

JOY. Your letters have been the most important thing in my life.

LEWIS. Oh dear.

JOY. But let's pretend I didn't say that. This is tea. This is England.

(THEY sit.)

LEWIS. So—how long have you been in the country?

JOY. Just over a week.

LEWIS. And what brings you to England?

JOY. Oh, well … I've wanted to come for some time.

WARNIE. So how do you find England, Mrs. Gresham?

JOY. Quiet. Extremely quiet. I would go so far as to say too quiet. The big mystery about the English is, where are they all? And why are they all so tired? Seriously. They don't talk. They don't move. All day they're timid and lethargic. What's going on?

LEWIS. Do you have an explanation?

JOY. I have a theory. My theory goes like this. The English are nocturnal creatures. They do their living at night. Somewhere in England there's this terrific party going on, all through the night, with everyone yelling and stomping and having one hell of a time. So all day, they're sleeping it off.

LEWIS. If only it were true. I'm afraid we don't have the famous energy of New York.

JOY. You can keep New York.

WARNIE. You're a New Yorker, are you, Mrs. Gresham?

JOY. Not anymore.

WARNIE. What does your husband do?

JOY Bill? Bill's a writer. Or he would be, if he ever wrote.

WARNIE. And you too, Jack tells me.

JOY. All in the past. You call him Jack?

LEWIS. From when I was four years old. I never liked the name Clive.

JOY. I wouldn't have thought of you as a Jack. But now that you say it, yes, you do look like a Jack.

LEWIS. What does a Jack look like?

JOY. Not at all spiritual.

LEWIS. Now I've disappointed you.

JOY. No. You're just becoming real, that's all.

LEWIS. I'm delighted to hear it.

DOUGLAS. Mom? Will he write in my book?

JOY. We'll have to ask him, won't we? Douglas has brought one of his Narnia books.

LEWIS. One of the Narnia books, have you really? What have you got there?

(DOUGLAS gives LEWIS his book.)

LEWIS. *The Magician's Nephew.* Very good. *(HE takes out a pen and writes on the flyleaf.)*

DOUGLAS. It's not true, is it?

LEWIS. That depends what you mean by true. It's a story.

DOUGLAS. Digory put on the magic ring, and it magicked him into a palace, where there was this beautiful queen, except she was really a witch, and he found a magic apple, and he brought it back for his mother, and she was very sick, and she got well again.

LEWIS. That sounds like a fair synopsis.

DOUGLAS. But it isn't true.

LEWIS. It's true in the story. There you are.

DOUGLAS. Can you do magic?

LEWIS. No. I'm afraid not.

DOUGLAS. Mom, can I be excused?

JOY. Is it all right if he runs around?

LEWIS. Runs around? I don't see why not.

JOY. Don't go too far, darling.

(DOUGLAS exits.)

JOY. All this "It isn't true" is his way of saying "I want it to be true." I was just like that at his age. I remember actually announcing to my parents that I had become an atheist.

LEWIS. You mean you secretly wanted to believe in God?

JOY. In something, at least. But I didn't know that then.

LEWIS. If I remember correctly, you've been through several phases. You were born a Jew, then you became a Communist, and then you converted to Christianity.

JOY. You remember correctly.

LEWIS. But you started with atheism?

JOY. No, I started with materialism. I had it all worked out by high school. Men are only apes.

LEWIS. Thanks very much.

JOY. Life is only an electrochemical reaction. Mind is only a set of conditioned reflexes. And, anyway, most people aren't rational like me. The universe is only matter. Matter is only energy. I forget what I said energy was only.

WARNIE. Extraordinary.

JOY. Oh, that was all a front. Somewhere deep inside there was somebody else.

LEWIS. The one who wrote the poems.

WARNIE. Ah? You're a poet, Mrs. Gresham?

JOY. Major Lewis, I know what you're thinking. You're thinking, God save us, she's going to start reciting.

WARNIE. I hope I'm not so bad-mannered.

JOY. No poetry at teatime. I know my manners too. But just to redeem myself a little, I must tell you that I did once win a national poetry award, which I shared with Robert Frost. You have heard of Robert Frost?

WARNIE. Yes. Absolutely.

JOY. But that's all in the past now.

LEWIS. Why is that?

JOY. Let's say, I've turned away from the mirror.

LEWIS. (*Intrigued.*) The mirror? Do you mean the reflection of yourself, or the reflection of the world?

JOY. The one being vanity, which is bad, the other being art, which is good?

LEWIS. Possibly.

JOY. I don't make that distinction. See yourself in the mirror, you're separate from yourself. See the world in the mirror, you're separate from the world. I don't want that separation anymore.

LEWIS. I could argue that art has quite the opposite effect. Great art breaks through that separateness, and lets us touch the very heart of reality.

JOY. Breaks through? That makes it sound as if art does all the work. I'd say we have to do the breaking through ourselves. Art teaches us how to know it when we see it, but art isn't it.

LEWIS. Oh, I see. Art is some sort of instruction manual for life, is it?

JOY. Hey! That's one of your favorite tricks, Mr. Lewis.

LEWIS. I beg your pardon?

JOY. You redescribe your opponent's argument with a dismissive image, and you think you've dismissed the argument.

LEWIS. (*Taken aback by her vigorous riposte, but he bows to the truth in her criticism.*) I stand corrected.

(*DOUGLAS re-enters, near the tea table, and stares at the bell that summons the waiter, obviously wanting to ring it.*)

DOUGLAS. Mom! Can I ring the bell?

JOY. No.

DOUGLAS. Can I have a glass of milk?

JOY. No. (*To Lewis.*) I really don't think we should take up any more of your time.

(ALL rise.)

LEWIS. It's extremely kind of you to come all this way. Warnie, I really should settle up.

(WARNIE rings the bell.)

LEWIS. Tell me, Mrs. Gresham, how long are you planning to be in England?

JOY. To the end of December.

LEWIS. Do you expect to be in Oxford again?

JOY. I don't know. I could be.

LEWIS. What do you say, Warnie? Could we rise to a pot of home-brewed tea?

WARNIE. I think we can manage that.

LEWIS. Given adequate warning, of course.

JOY. Thank you. I'd like that.

LEWIS. Well, I'd better see what the damage is.

(The WAITER enters, and LEWIS goes to pay the bill.)

JOY. Major Lewis, I must rely on you to tell me if I take up too much of your brother's time.

WARNIE. I'm sure you have time pressures of your own, Mrs. Gresham.

JOY. Oh, sure. Some.

(WARNIE and JOY make their way to the exit.)

JOY. Your brother has given me so much. Through his writing, I mean. I think it might surprise you to know just how much.

WARNIE. Mrs. Gresham, everything surprises me.

(THEY exit.

LEWIS is about to follow when HE sees DOUGLAS, who is still hanging around the bell.)

LEWIS. Douglas, do you remember the bell in the book?

DOUGLAS. Yes. And the queen was sitting in a stone chair, and she was very beautiful, and she didn't move or even breathe. But she wasn't dead.

LEWIS. No. She was waiting.

DOUGLAS. Waiting for someone to ring the bell.

LEWIS. Do you remember the writing on the pillar beneath the bell? "Make your choice, adventurous stranger. Strike the bell, and bide the danger."

(MUSIC begins: the music of the magic world.)

DOUGLAS. Can I?

LEWIS. It'll break the spell. It'll wake the queen.

DOUGLAS. I don't care.

LEWIS. All right, then.

(DOUGLAS rings the BELL.

The LIGHTS change. The screen rises. The door of the giant wardrobe slowly opens to reveal a magical infinite space beyond: a child's vision of Paradise.

DOUGLAS walks toward the opening wardrobe door, as if hypnotized.

LEWIS watches.

DOUGLAS enters the magic world, and the great door closes behind him. The MUSIC fades. The brief glimpse of another world is over.

The LIGHTS change again. The set is once more the study at The Kilns.

WARNIE enters, carrying Christmas paper chains. LEWIS joins him, and together THEY hang the paper chains.)

WARNIE. Here you are, Jack.

LEWIS. Thank you, Warnie. It's only a cup of tea, Warnie. She won't stay long.

WARNIE. I didn't say a word.

(THEY work in silence for a few moments.)

LEWIS. At least one can talk to her.

WARNIE. Listen to her.

LEWIS. You think she's going to make a nuisance of herself, don't you?

WARNIE. I'm sure you know what you're doing, Jack.

LEWIS. She sails back to New York at the end of the month. One can be so much more friendly to people who can't stay long.

WARNIE. What about the boy? What did you write in his book, by the way?

LEWIS. "The magic never ends."

WARNIE. You don't think that's overstating things a little?

LEWIS. He's only a child.

WARNIE. He'll ask for his money back later.

LEWIS. You know what she said about Douglas, how "It isn't true" is his way of saying "I want it to be true"? Don't you think that was perceptive?

WARNIE. I wonder what her husband thinks of her running round England like this.

LEWIS. This isn't the Middle Ages, Warnie.

WARNIE. She is American, of course.

LEWIS. And a poet.

WARNIE. She'll make you listen to one of her poems. I bet you ten shillings to sixpence. Then she'll say to you, "How do you like it, Mr. Lewis?" And you'll be stumped.

LEWIS. I shall say, "Only you could have written that."

WARNIE. "A distinctive voice."

(The DOORBELL rings.)

LEWIS. Absolutely. There they are.

WARNIE. It is a three-line whip?

LEWIS. Not at all.

(LEWIS exits and can be heard greeting Joy and Douglas offstage. WARNIE finishes the decorations.)

LEWIS. *(Offstage.)* You found us. Welcome.

JOY. *(Offstage.)* Hello! Take your coat off, Douglas. *(JOY enters and looks around, openly curious.)* Hello. Oh, look at that.

(DOUGLAS, following her, goes straight to a bookcase and starts taking out books. LEWIS too enters.)

WARNIE. Mrs. Gresham, if you'll excuse me. I'm going to leave Jack to entertain you.

JOY. Oh. Good to see you again, Major Lewis. *(To Lewis.)* Do you mind Douglas looking at your books?

LEWIS. That's what books are for.

WARNIE. Jack is particularly hoping you'll introduce him to your poetry.

(WARNIE gives Lewis a meaningful glance and exits.)

JOY. Are you?

LEWIS. I'd be interested to know what you write.

JOY. Wrote. All in the past. *(SHE takes off her hat and coat and gloves and walks around the room, examining it in more detail.)*

(DOUGLAS has curled up in a corner with a book.)

JOY. How long have you and your brother lived here?

LEWIS. Would you believe, for over twenty years.

JOY. Good heavens! No wonder it's so comfortable.

LEWIS. My friends call it The Midden. They say if I move the bookcases, the walls will fall down. Make yourself at home, and I'll see if I can summon up some tea. *(HE exits to get the tea.)*

JOY. What have you got there?

DOUGLAS. *The Lion, the Witch, and the Wardrobe.*

JOY. The best. Be careful with that. It's probably Mr. Lewis's first copy. *(JOY goes to the desk to examine the books piled there.)*

LEWIS. (*Re-enters with a tray of tea.*) As you see, I'm all prepared.

JOY. Sir Philip Sidney. Sir Thomas Wyatt. You like your poets to have titles.

LEWIS. I'm working on *English Literature in the Sixteenth Century*, excluding drama. For *OHEL*.

JOY. Oh hell?

LEWIS. *The Oxford History of English Literature.*

JOY. Sixteenth century. You got the easy one.

LEWIS. You think so?

JOY. Well, who is there? Spenser. If you cheat, you can squeeze Shakespeare in at the end.

LEWIS. Excluding drama.

JOY. *Venus and Adonis*? *The Rape of Lucrece*? They must be fifteen ninety-something.

LEWIS. You're quite right.

JOY. Of course, you do have Knox's *The First Blast of the Trumpet Against the Monstrous Regiment of Women*. That is what I call one hell of a title.

LEWIS. Do you really? And, what did you call your book of poems?

JOY. *Letters to a Comrade. (SHE mimes an exaggerated yawn.)*

LEWIS. Do you remember any of them?

JOY. Oh, you don't want to hear—

LEWIS. No, no. Come on.

JOY. Okay, let's get it over with. Let's see ... Here's one I wrote when I was twenty-two. Spanish Civil War. It's called "Snow in Madrid."

LEWIS. In your own time.

(JOY recites, a little self-consciously, watching Lewis's reaction as she does so.)

JOY.
   Softly, so casual,
   Lovely, so light, so light.
   The cruel sky lets fall
   Something one does not fight.

   Men before perishing
   See with unwounded eye
   For once, a gentle thing
   Fall from the sky.

(LEWIS says nothing. It is not what he expected.)

JOY. Embarrassed, huh? Well, buddy, you asked for it, you get out of it.

LEWIS. No. I'm touched.

JOY. Touched? Okay, that'll do. That's about its level. When was I ever in Madrid? The answer is, never.

LEWIS. Personal experience isn't everything.

JOY. You don't think so?

LEWIS. I've never been to Madrid, but I know it's there.

JOY How about Narnia? Ever been there?

LEWIS. Now, that's an interesting question. I'm not sure. I suppose I've sent surrogates of myself there. Children.

JOY. Yourself as a child.

LEWIS. Something like that.

JOY. It is different when you feel something for yourself. And it's a lot different when it hurts.

LEWIS. Just because something hurts, it doesn't make it more true. Or even more significant.

JOY. No. I guess not.

LEWIS. Douglas. There's some orange squash and some fruit cake, if you want it.

(DOUGLAS takes the glass of squash and the cake.)

LEWIS. I'm not saying pain is purposeless, or even neutral. Not at all. But to find meaning in pain, there has to be something else. Pain is a tool. If you like, pain is God's mega—

JOY. God's megaphone to rouse a deaf world.

LEWIS. How embarrassing. You know my writing too well.

JOY. I know it because I've read it and reread it. I knew you pretty well before we met.

LEWIS. Ah, but you had not had the Personal Experience.

JOY. Mr. Lewis—Listen, I can't go on calling you Mr. Lewis, it makes me feel like a kid. Can I call you Jack?

LEWIS. Of course you can.

JOY. Jack. I'm Joy. *(SHE shakes his hand.)*

LEWIS. Hello, Joy. How do you do. Well, there … that's that.

JOY. So—Jack. Have you ever been really hurt?

LEWIS. You don't give up, do you?

JOY. I'm sorry. I withdraw the question. What do you do for Christmas?

LEWIS. Oh, much as last year. Roast turkey, Christmas pud, far too much to drink. How about you?

JOY. We haven't decided. Some lucky English hotel. That should be a new experience.

LEWIS. Then home for the New Year.

JOY. Home. Yes.

(This thought quietens JOY. There follows a short silence.)

LEWIS. I have been really hurt, you know. The first time is always the worst. That was when my mother died.

JOY. How old were you?

LEWIS. Eight.

JOY. Old enough to hurt.

LEWIS. Oh yes. It was the end of my world. I remember my father in tears. Voices all over the house. Doors shutting and opening. It was a big house—all long, empty corridors. I remember, I had the toothache. I wanted my mother to come to me. I cried for her to come, but she didn't come.

JOY. What was it?

LEWIS. It was cancer. It followed the usual course. An operation. An apparent recovery. A return of the disease. Increasing pain. Death.

JOY. And after death? Did you believe in heaven, when you were a child? Did you believe you'd meet her again?

LEWIS. No. She was gone. That was all.

JOY. And you went somewhere secret to cry?

LEWIS. I went somewhere secret. I didn't cry.

(THEY both fall silent again. JOY, feeling she has come close to him, is about to continue at this more personal level when HE turns away.)

LEWIS. Douglas. There's some more orange squash if you'd like.

JOY. No thanks, Jack. We should go.

LEWIS. Go? You only just got here. Well, I'm frightfully glad you both came.

JOY. I'm frightfully glad you asked us. *(SHE rises.)* Douglas. Book back. Coat on.

(DOUGLAS does as he is told.)

LEWIS. He doesn't make a fuss, does he?

JOY. Douglas and I understand each other.

LEWIS. Joy, I don't like to think of you Christmasing in a hotel. Why don't you both come here? You'd be very welcome.

JOY. No, no. You don't want strangers rampaging all over your house.

LEWIS. I'll have to ask Warnie, of course. But speaking for myself, I would welcome the company.

JOY. It's very kind of you, Jack. You ask Warnie. But we can look after ourselves, I promise you. We're very independent, aren't we, Douglas?

(JOY and DOUGLAS exit as she speaks. LEWIS follows, speaking as HE too exits.)

LEWIS. You'd be doing me a kindness. I'm sure Warnie will be delighted.

*(WARNIE, RILEY, OAKLEY, and HARRINGTON enter.
This is a pre-Christmas drinks party. RILEY gazes at
the Christmas decorations.*
LEWIS enters with a plate of cocktail sausages.)

RILEY. What I resent about Christmas is the general presumption of good will. I feel no good will towards my fellow men. I feel ill will.

LEWIS. It's got nothing to do with how you feel, Christopher. Feelings are far too unreliable.

RILEY. Maybe so, Jack, but they're very close to me. I'm very attached to my feelings. I won't hear a word against them. They're easily hurt.

HARRINGTON. I'm afraid Christmas is something of a lost cause, Jack.

LEWIS. That depends on how it's presented. If you tell people it's about peace in the world, and being kind to the poor and needy, then naturally nobody listens.

RILEY. Aha, the archcommunicator in action! Give us the sales pitch, Jack.

LEWIS. "Virgin Has Sex with Omnipotent Alien— Gives Birth to God."

RILEY. I've always thought the incarnation proves that God has a severely limited intellect. Who'd choose, voluntarily, to be human, when you have the option of staying safely divine?

LEWIS. Think of the magic, Christopher. The birth of a helpless, squealing creature who is also God. An all-powerful baby. Doesn't that satisfy your taste for the peculiar? It's the coming of new life in the heart of winter, when all the land is dead. The snow falls, and the trees are bare. All but one tree, which bears fruit. That's real magic.

HARRINGTON. I think you're a little hard on the poor and needy, Jack. No room at the inn, remember?

WARNIE. Jack's invited them to stay with us.

RILEY. Really, Jack?

HARRINGTON. Who?

WARNIE. Mother and child. They're upstairs.

LEWIS. Mrs. Gresham and her son. They're spending Christmas with us.

RILEY. Well, Jack, you have succeeded in surprising me. Who is Mrs. Gresham?

LEWIS. Wait and see.

WARNIE. She's an American.

RILEY. Curiouser and curiouser.

JOY. (*Enters.*) Merry Christmas!

LEWIS. Ah, Joy. Let me introduce you. Dr. Maurice Oakley. The Reverend Harry Harrington. Professor Christopher Riley. Mrs. Joy Gresham.

HARRINGTON. Delighted to meet you, Mrs. Gresham.

RILEY. Mrs. Gresham, how opportune. I understand you're from the United States of America.

JOY. Yes, I am.

RILEY. Then perhaps you can satisfy my curiosity on a small matter. Jack's children's stories are published in America, they tell me. Are they or are they not in translation?

JOY. I don't understand.

RILEY. *The Lion, the Witch, and the Clothes-Closet?*

LEWIS. Behave yourself, Christopher.

RILEY. Forgive me, Jack. Success breeds envy, as ever.

LEWIS. I don't know what you call success. Most of my friends treat my children's books as a form of juvenile dementia.

JOY. Have you read any of them, Professor Riley?

RILEY. Jack has read extracts aloud to me. It is one of his tests of friendship.

JOY. He's been reading me Sir Philip Sidney.

RILEY. Is that more bearable?

JOY. Bearable? Sidney's glorious.

(Her unselfconscious enthusiasm clearly delights LEWIS.)

LEWIS. He is, isn't he?

JOY. He has this inspired image of Desire, capital D, as a baby that won't stop bawling. "Sleep, baby mine, Desire, Nurse Beauty singeth—"

LEWIS. "Thy cries, O baby, set mine head on aching." I'm afraid Sidney was rather down on desire.

JOY. Babies just yell until they get what they want. That's what I love about the image. It's precise. Nowadays, poets are so lazy.

LEWIS. You sound like me, Joy. You're supposed to be dragging me kicking into the twentieth century.

JOY. I've been force-feeding Jack T. S. Eliot, but even Eliot can be lazy. "When the evening is spread out against the sky, Like a patient etherised upon a table." What kind of image is that? He could just as easily have written, "Like a cocktail sausage upon a tray."

RILEY. *(Beginning to feel excluded.)* Congratulations, Jack. You seem to have found a soul mate.

LEWIS. I thought you believed we didn't have souls, Christopher.

RILEY. Well now, you see, I regard the soul as an essentially feminine accessory. "Anima." Quite different from "animus," the male variant. This is how I explain the otherwise puzzling difference between the sexes. Where men have intellect, women have soul.

JOY. Professor Riley, as you know, I'm an American, and different cultures have different modes of discourse. I need a little guidance here. Are you being offensive, or merely stupid?

(LEWIS, HARRINGTON, OAKLEY, and WARNIE laugh.
RILEY, rather put out, but trying to laugh it off pulls a face at Lewis.)

LEWIS. Serves you right, Christopher. Don't be such a bully.

RILEY. I feel like calling for police protection. Where on earth did you find her?

HARRINGTON. Tell me, Mrs. Gresham, how do you find England?

JOY. Cold. Dull.

RILEY. How very perceptive. How original.

JOY. And I don't much care for the weather, either. Will you excuse me, Jack? Reverend Harrington, Dr. Oakley, Professor Riley, it's been my pleasure.

(JOY leaves them but does not exit. SHE goes into the outer set, which we understand is another room, and

*there rereads an airmail letter that arrived earlier in the
day.
Her brisk departure has the effect of breaking up the little
party.)*

LEWIS. *(Takes up the plate of cocktail sausages.)* Oh,
come on, let's finish these up, shall we?

HARRINGTON. I don't think I could, Jack.

WARNIE. I'll take those, Jack. We'll heat them up for
supper. *(WARNIE exits.)*

LEWIS. I shall look forward to that.

(RILEY takes LEWIS aside.)

RILEY. Jack, she's simply ghastly. You must get rid
of her.

LEWIS. Oh, come off it, Christopher. Just because she
bit you back.

RILEY. Good lord, I don't mind that. But she's got her
hooks into you. You must see that.

LEWIS. Christopher, she's a married woman, and she's
a committed Christian. That may not warm the cockles of
your heathen heart, but it does mean she's unlikely to have
adulterous designs on me.

RILEY. Never send to know for whom the wedding bell
tolls, Jack.

LEWIS. Look at you. All worked up over nothing. Fear
not, she's harmless. And after Christmas, she sails back to
New York.

RILEY. Beware Christmas, Jack. Look what happened
to Scrooge.

LEWIS. Happy Christmas, Christopher.

RILEY. Easy to say, Jack. Easy to say. (*RILEY exits.*)

HARRINGTON. Thanks for the drinks, Jack. Happy Christmas.

LEWIS. Are you off? Happy Christmas, Harry.

OAKLEY. Happy Christmas, Jack.

LEWIS. Good night, Maurice.

(HARRINGTON and OAKLEY exit.

LEWIS crosses the stage to join JOY as she stands reading her letter.)

LEWIS. You mustn't mind about Christopher. It's nothing personal. Just how he is.

JOY. It's not important.

LEWIS. (*Realizes that something in her letter is absorbing her attention.*) Letter from home?

JOY. Yes.

LEWIS. Bad news?

JOY. In a way.

LEWIS. Anything I can do?

JOY. I'm not sure. *(SHE falls silent.)*

LEWIS. What is it?

JOY. If I was back home and this was happening, I'd write to you to tell me what to do. I could say it in a letter.

LEWIS. That's easy. *(HE takes a chair and turns it so that its back is to Joy then sits where she can't see his face.)* Tell me like a letter. Off you go. "Dear Mr. Lewis …"

JOY. (*Falls in with his suggestion, at first tentatively, then with increasing feeling and fluency.*) Dear Mr. Lewis. My husband has just written to me to tell me that he's fallen in love with another woman. Her name is Renee. He wants me to give him a divorce, so that he'll be free to marry her. *(SHE takes up the letter and reads from it.)* "Renee and I are in love, and have been since about the middle of August. If it had not been for our love I could not have come through this summer with as little anguish as I have, for things have been rough financially." Maybe you wonder if I knew about Renee. The answer is no. But Renee is not the first.

LEWIS. Do you love your husband?

JOY. I don't know how to answer that one. Bill's very talented, he wants to do right by everyone, he's a good man at heart, and I guess I love him. Bill's a drunk, he sleeps around a lot, he's sometimes violent, and I guess I haven't loved him for years. Once he broke a bottle over Douglas's head. Two days later he said, "When have you ever known me do an unkind thing?" He's worn me out. That's the truth of it. The only thing that's new is he wants a divorce.

LEWIS. I had no idea.

JOY. How could you? People never know about other people's lives. You have to live it to know it. Sorry. You don't agree with that.

LEWIS. Contrary to popular opinion, I don't know everything.

JOY. *(Recovers herself slowly.)* A lot of good things have come out of my life with Bill. We were happy at the beginning. And there's Douglas. And there's something else, too. Something that happened to me, that was very important, that in a strange way I owe to Bill. Something I don't talk about. But I'd like to tell you. If you don't mind.

LEWIS. Tell me.

JOY. It only lasted thirty seconds, maybe less, but it changed everything for me. I've been turning into a different person ever since.

LEWIS. What happened?

JOY. We were living in Westchester County. Bill was working in the city. One day he phoned from his office to say he was losing control of his mind and that he wasn't ever coming home. Bang went the phone down. That was it. I had a small baby. I was alone. I had no idea what to do. I phoned everyone I knew. They hadn't seen Bill. I put the baby to bed, and I waited. He didn't come. I didn't know if he was dead or alive. Round about midnight, I broke down. I never felt so helpless in my life. The baby was upstairs asleep. I was downstairs. I was crying. Then there was someone else in the room. Just for a few seconds, maybe half a minute. But I knew it was a real person. More real than real. So real that everything else was like shadows. I said something, I've no idea what. I guess I was just saying, Okay then. Okay. *(SHE looks up at Lewis and sees that HE understands.)*

LEWIS. And tell me, what news of your husband?

JOY. Bill came home three days later. I told him. He said, "I wish God would come to me." I'll say this for Bill, he has an open mind. He just can't keep any one thing in it for long.

LEWIS. Are you going to go back?

JOY. What about the divorce, Jack?

LEWIS. Marriage isn't just a legal contract.

JOY. We'd still be married, in the eyes of God.

LEWIS. Yes.

JOY. And I wouldn't be free to marry anyone else.

LEWIS. No.

JOY. No, I know. I've read your writings on the subject. Many times.

(LEWIS says nothing. He can't tell her what she wants to hear.)

JOY. So, that's it, I guess.

LEWIS. Joy, tell me. Is this woman actually living with your husband in your house?

JOY. Yes. I guess so.

LEWIS. And that's where you're going back to?

JOY. Where else can I go?

LEWIS. And later?

JOY. I don't know. I'm sorry to burden you with all this. It's not your problem. Don't worry. I'll be alright. I always have been.

LEWIS. I wish there was some way I could help.

JOY. There is.

LEWIS. *(Looks up, almost frightened to hear what she has to say.)* Yes?

JOY. Be my friend.

LEWIS. Well, I'm that already.

JOY. I know. Thank you. I'm just going to go upstairs now ... *(On the point of further tears, JOY hurries out.)*

(LEWIS looks after her for a moment or two. Then HE too rises and exits, in a different direction.

The LIGHTING changes. It is morning.

WARNIE enters, carrying the breakfast tray as he did earlier, and his newspaper. HE pours out two cups of coffee.

LEWIS enters, carrying the morning mail.)

WARNIE. Morning, Jack.

LEWIS. Morning. Two for you. *(HE sits at his desk. The bachelor routine has returned.)*

(After a while, and without taking their eyes off their reading, THEY have one of their noncommittal conversations.)

WARNIE. You miss her, don't you?

LEWIS. Things are quieter now.

WARNIE. I'm afraid I'm not much of a talker.

LEWIS. One of your many virtues, Warnie.

WARNIE. Is she coming back?

LEWIS. No, no. Why should she come back?

(An interval of silence.)

LEWIS. I haven't really thanked you, Warnie.

WARNIE. What for?

LEWIS. You've been very tolerant. Very considerate.

WARNIE. Any friend of yours, Jack.

LEWIS. I know.

(The DOORBELL rings. LEWIS calls out, without rising or even turning his attention from what he is writing.)

LEWIS. That'll be Christopher. Door's open, Christopher.

(WARNIE looks at his watch, a little surprised at this early visit, and then goes back to reading the paper.

*RILEY enters, carrying a typescript. HE looks around with
mock trepidation.)*

RILEY. Is it safe to come in? La belle dame sans
merci? *(HE pronounces "dame" in the American manner.)*

LEWIS. Now, Christopher, you know perfectly well
that she went back to New York ages ago.

RILEY. *(Puts the typescript on Lewis's desk before
him.)* Tom's latest, as promised. The only copy.

LEWIS. Is it up to scratch?

RILEY. Not bad. If he wasn't a friend, I'd say pretty
good. *(HE goes to Warnie.)* Morning, Warnie.

WARNIE. Morning, Christopher.

RILEY. *(Turns and remarks to Lewis.)* Just as well,
perhaps, Jack.

LEWIS. What is?

RILEY. The return of the native.

LEWIS. What are you trying to say?

RILEY. You know how people talk.

LEWIS. To be honest, Christopher, I don't know and I
don't care. A like-minded man and woman are entitled to be
friends, it seems to me. I don't see why I should disqualify
half the human race just because they're also available for
other purposes.

RILEY. I won't quarrel with that. Friendship forever.

LEWIS. It's all love or sex these days. Friendship is
almost as quaint and outdated a notion as chastity. Soon
friends will be like the elves and the pixies—fabulous
mythical creatures from a distant past.

RILEY. Too optimistic, Jack. Friendship will be made
illegal, clearly. "The accused has been found guilty of gross

public friendship. I hereby pass sentence of five years'
marriage, with no remission."

*(THEY chuckle. WARNIE puts down his paper and rises
from his chair.)*

WARNIE. No news, of course. Never is.

RILEY. Shall we see you in hall, Warnie? Like old
times?

WARNIE. Like old times, Christopher. Why not?
(WARNIE exits.)

*(RILEY sits down in his chair and picks up the
newspaper.)*

LEWIS. *(Becomes reflective.)* Tell me something,
Christopher. How can I put this? Would you say that you
were ... content?

RILEY. I am as I am. The world is as it is. My
contentment or otherwise has very little to do with it.

LEWIS. You don't ever feel a sense of waste?

RILEY. Of course. All life is waste. Remember, I don't
have your faith in divine recycling.

LEWIS. I've always found this a trying time of the
year. The leaves not yet out. Mud everywhere you go. The
frosty mornings gone, and the sunny mornings not yet
come. The air dank and unhealthy. Give me blizzards and
frozen pipes, but not this nothing time. Not this waiting
room of a world.

RILEY. May will come, Jack. And June. And July.

LEWIS. And I have two books to finish, and six talks to write, and letters, letters, letters. *(HE turns to the work waiting on his desk.)*

(RILEY rises from his chair and watches him with some sympathy, understanding him better than his friend realizes. Then HE exits.

LEWIS finds it difficult to concentrate, but after a few moments HE gets into the way of it.

As he works, JOY enters. HE does not see her.

SHE stands still, watching Lewis work, but does not speak.

LEWIS becomes aware that he is not alone. HE raises his head, listening without turning around.)

JOY. Remember me, Jack?

LEWIS. Joy! *(HE turns around and sees her.)* What are you doing here?

JOY The door was open.

LEWIS. But…?

JOY. We live here now. Douglas and I.

LEWIS. Here? In Oxford?

JOY. Yes, but don't worry. We have our own house. We'll be no trouble at all.

(LEWIS stares at her, still too stunned to be polite.)

JOY. Want a cup of tea?

LEWIS. Yes. Thank you very much. I'd love one.

JOY. Then you're going to have to make it. This is your house.

LEWIS. Of course. Yes. I'm sorry, Joy, I'm a little confused. Why didn't you write?

JOY. What for? To ask permission?

LEWIS. No, no. But ... when did you decide this? How did you find a house? How was it all arranged?

JOY. And what have I done with Bill? We're divorced. No more Bill. No more America.

LEWIS. I see.

JOY. Do you mind?

LEWIS. Why should I mind?

JOY. I don't know. You might.

LEWIS. No. I don't mind.

JOY. That's alright, then.

(THEY walk forward, out of the study. The screen falls.)

JOY. So tell me the news.

LEWIS. What news?

JOY. Don't tell me that time has stood still since I've been away.

LEWIS. Gone by at a slow amble, perhaps. I may be offered a chair at Cambridge, if you call that news. Professor of medieval and Renaissance literature.

JOY. Will you take it?

LEWIS. Probably.

JOY. You'd leave Oxford?

LEWIS. Only to teach. I'd go on living here. Cambridge is a chilly sort of town.

JOY. So you won't be moving out just as I move in? *(SHE makes a joke of this, but SHE is secretly relieved that he is not leaving Oxford.)*

LEWIS. (*Looks at her with affection.*) I really am very—very surprised to see you, you know.

JOY. I think you're overdoing the surprise a bit, Jack. I wasn't dead. I was only in America.

LEWIS. Yes, of course. But you see, I've been thinking about—(*HE hesitates to say it, then decides he will.*) Oh, alright, I've been thinking about you.

JOY. I am honored.

LEWIS. There we are. I was thinking about you. And all of a sudden there you were.

JOY. Here I am. Present tense. Present, and tense.

LEWIS. I really am very glad to see you again, Joy.

JOY. Thank you, Jack.

(He has gone a little further than he intended and changes the subject to the safer, more neutral matter now facing them)

LEWIS. Moving house is a sort of revolution, I always think. The old order is overthrown, a new order waits to be born. One wakes up facing a strange way, one's books are all in strange places, and there's nowhere to hang one's dressing gown.

(In the course of this speech, the screen rises to reveal Joy's house. It is empty but for packing cases.)

JOY. When did you last move house?

LEWIS. Twenty-five years ago. Thank God that's over.

(JOY laughs. SHE goes to work on the packing cases. LEWIS looks about the room.)

JOY. I don't know why I brought all this stuff.

LEWIS. What is it?

JOY. My uncollected works. How can I have written all this stuff?

LEWIS. I'm sure it's nothing to be ashamed of.

JOY. You haven't read it. Nor will you.

LEWIS. What can I do to help?

JOY. Books into shelves.

LEWIS. Books into shelves. Any particular order?

JOY. Put them anywhere they'll fit. I'll sort them out later.

(LEWIS takes the books and starts reading one of them. JOY watches him.)

JOY. Jack, are you sure you want to do this?

LEWIS. I said I'd help.

(THEY work on in silence for a few moments.)

LEWIS. Joy, how does Bill feel about you coming to live in England?

JOY I don't think he likes it. On the other hand, he can only afford to give me sixty dollars a month, and England's cheaper.

LEWIS. How much is that? It doesn't sound enough.

JOY. We'll manage.

LEWIS. If you find things are getting tight, you will let me know, won't you?

JOY. I don't want to take your money, Jack.

LEWIS. Don't be silly. That's what friends are for.

JOY. We are friends, aren't we?

LEWIS. We most certainly are.

(JOY's attention is caught by a newspaper in which her possessions have been packed. The headline announces Princess Margaret's dramatic "duty before love" decision not to marry Group-Captain Peter Townsend.)

JOY. "Should Princess Margaret have followed the dictates of her heart? ... Group-Captain Peter Townsend's lips are sealed, but his hands are shaking ... She chose duty before love." So what do you think about the heartbreak princess?

LEWIS. The dictates of her heart! It almost sounds like a higher authority, doesn't it? All it means is, doing what she feels like doing.

JOY. I knew you'd be on the side of duty.

LEWIS. I don't pretend it's an easy decision.

JOY. Easy it's not. *(SHE returns to the business of unpacking.)*

LEWIS. It's a big change for you, this.

JOY. England?

LEWIS. Yes.

JOY. If it turns out to be a mistake, I'll have lost very little. But I do hope it works out for Douglas.

LEWIS. What made you decide?

JOY. I had to go somewhere. And I like England.

LEWIS. And it's cheaper.

JOY. I like Oxford.

LEWIS. All those warm-hearted dons, with their love of female company.

JOY. I can handle that.

LEWIS. The balmy English weather.

JOY. I like the way Oxford's been here a long time. Not everything is the impulse of the moment. I like being among educated people. And I like living in the same town as you. Do you mind?

LEWIS. My dear Joy, I don't own Oxford.

JOY. Do you mind?

LEWIS. Of course I don't mind. Why should I?

JOY. You know what I mean, Jack.

LEWIS. I'm delighted to have you as a neighbor.

(SHE looks at him.)

LEWIS. Why are you looking at me like that?

JOY. Like what?

LEWIS. As if I'm lying to you. Why should I lie to you? I mean what I say.

JOY. I know that. But you don't say it all, do you?

LEWIS. One can't say it all. It would take too long.

JOY. Alright, Jack. But I trust you to tell me anything I need to know.

(Again, SHE returns to the unpacking. LEWIS puzzles over what she has just said.)

LEWIS. What sort of thing do you need to know?

JOY. I want to stay friends with you, Jack. I need to know anything that would make that hard for you.

LEWIS. I see.

JOY. We might as well know where we are.

LEWIS. Best to have things out in the open, you think?

JOY. That's how I like it.

LEWIS. You never can really tell what's going on between people, can you? People jump to conclusions. Sometimes it makes me quite angry the way people aren't allowed to be ... well, just friends.

JOY. Like us, you mean.

LEWIS. Like us. I don't mean to say that friendship is a small thing. As a matter of fact, I rate it as one of this life's most precious gifts.

JOY. But ...

LEWIS. But it shouldn't be turned into a watered-down version of something it is not.

JOY. Such as ...

LEWIS. Such as, well, to give you one example, romantic love. Which nowadays is just about the only emotion men and women are permitted to feel for each other. Though that's not to say that friendship isn't, in its way—

JOY. A kind of love.

LEWIS. A kind of love. I knew you'd understand.

JOY. I understand better than that, Jack. You are a bachelor and I am a divorced woman. Some people might suppose you to have some idea of marrying me. You have no such idea. I am to have no false expectations. You want to have this "out in the open" because you care about me and don't want me to be hurt. Have I understood you correctly?

LEWIS. You are extraordinary. I really don't know what to say.

JOY. It's okay. I just said it. Wasn't so hard, was it?

LEWIS. I'm not used to this ... whatever it is.

JOY. Naming names. That's all it is.

LEWIS. Yes.

JOY. So now you don't need to be afraid of me, do you?

LEWIS. Good Lord, I was never afraid of you, Joy.

(SHE looks at him. HE shrugs and smiles.)

JOY. I really do appreciate your help, Jack.

LEWIS. The least I can do. Look, I'm sure there are far more substantial ways I can help, that you're not telling me about.

JOY. I don't want to exhaust your good will.

LEWIS. No fear of that. I think it grows by being drawn on.

JOY. There is something you could do which would help me enormously. But if I asked for something and you can't give it, I want you to just say no. I mean, just no. No guilt, no evasion, no running away.

LEWIS. I hope so. I don't think you'd ask for anything beyond my power to give.

JOY. No. It's not beyond your power to give ...

LEWIS. So, there's something in particular, isn't there?

JOY. Yes, there is. There is something you could do that would help me a great deal.

LEWIS. I think I know what it is. You want me to put the kettle on.

JOY. *(Laughs.)* Come on—I'll tell you about it in the kitchen.

(SHE exits. LEWIS exits.
The screen falls.

WARNIE enters, with a deck chair, and settles down to read.
LEWIS enters with a deck chair of his own and does likewise.
After a few moments.)

WARNIE. So she's settled over here for good, has she?
LEWIS. Who knows? For the foreseeable future.
WARNIE. Why Oxford?
LEWIS. Why not Oxford? Dreaming spires, and so forth.
WARNIE. You know how it looks, don't you, Jack?
LEWIS. I know.

(Neither of them has taken his nose out of his book. There follows a short silence. Then.)

LEWIS. She's a good friend to me, Warnie. That's all.
WARNIE. *(Nods.)* Is that how she sees it?
LEWIS. I wouldn't presume to raise the matter.
WARNIE. No. Of course not.

(Another short silence.)

LEWIS. Oh, Warnie. There is something you should know.
WARNIE. What's that, Jack?
LEWIS. I've agreed to marry her.
WARNIE. You have?
LEWIS. Yes. Seemed like the right thing to do.
WARNIE. You astound me. No, I mean—

LEWIS. It's alright, Warnie. Nothing's going to change. I'm not really going to marry Joy.

WARNIE. You're not?

LEWIS. What I have agreed to do is extend my British citizenship to her, so that she can go on living in England.

WARNIE. By marrying her.

LEWIS. Only technically.

WARNIE. You're marrying Joy technically?

LEWIS. A true marriage is a declaration before God, not before some government official. Joy will keep her own name. She will go on living in her own house. We will go on living here exactly as before. No one will even know the marriage has taken place, apart from you, Somerset House, and the Department of Immigration. It is nothing more than a bureaucratic formality. See you at tea.

(In the course of this speech LEWIS has risen and taken up his chair. HE now exits.
A clap of THUNDER is heard.)

WARNIE. Oh, blast. *(WARNIE exits.)*

(The screen rises to reveal a registry office, where JOY waits, before a REGISTRAR.
A WITNESS stands behind JOY, a.CLERIC sits by the REGISTRAR.
WARNIE joins them. LEWIS enters, hurriedly and late, carrying a pile of books.)

LEWIS. I'm so sorry.

REGISTRAR. Mr. Lewis. Please be seated. *(HE opens a book and reads from it.)* We'll proceed at once. Before you are joined in matrimony, I have to remind you of the solemn and binding character of the vows you are about to make. Marriage according to the law of this country is the union of one man with one woman, voluntarily entered into for life, to the exclusion of all others. Now we proceed to the declarations. If you'd both stand. Mr. Lewis, if you'll repeat after me. "I call upon these persons here present ..."

LEWIS. (*Speaks in an unduly clear voice.*) I call upon these persons here present ...

REGISTRAR. "... to witness that I, Clive Staples Lewis ..."

LEWIS. ... to witness that I, Clive Staples Lewis ...

REGISTRAR. "... do take thee, Helen Joy Davidman ..."

LEWIS. ... do take thee, Helen Joy Davidman ...

REGISTRAR. "... to be my lawful wedded wife."

LEWIS. ... to be my lawful wedded wife.

REGISTRAR. Miss Davidman, if you'll repeat after me. "I call upon these persons here present ..."

JOY. (*JOY's responses are more muted.*) I call upon these persons here present ...

REGISTRAR. "... to witness that I, Helen Joy Davidman..."

JOY. ... to witness that I, Helen Joy Davidman ...

REGISTRAR. "... do take thee, Clive Staples Lewis ..."

JOY. ... do take thee, Clive Staples Lewis ...

REGISTRAR. "... to be my lawful wedded husband."

JOY. ... to be my lawful wedded husband.

REGISTRAR. Do we have a ring?

(LEWIS and JOY speak together.)

> LEWIS. No.
> JOY. No
> LEWIS. Sorry.
> JOY. Sorry.

(The whole affair is very awkward and embarrassing.)

REGISTRAR. No ring. Very well. If you'll please both sign the register. Before you sign, be careful to check that all the details are exactly correct.

(JOY signs the register quickly. LEWIS studies it carefully before signing.
WARNIE signs the register, as do the WITNESS, the REGISTRAR, and finally the CLERK. The CLERK puts the certificate in an envelope.)

CLERK. Mrs. Lewis. Mrs. Lewis.

(JOY comes and takes the envelope.)

REGISTRAR. May I be the first to congratulate you, and wish you every happiness in your life together.

LEWIS. Well, do you know, that's most kind of you. Good day.

(The REGISTRAR exits.
LEWIS, JOY, and WARNIE walk downstage, and the screen falls behind them. THEY have come out into rain.)

JOY. What a terrible day.

LEWIS. That's that, then.

JOY. Can I invite you both back for a drink?

LEWIS. I simply can't, Joy. Please forgive me, but I must get back to work. You know how it is.

JOY. Of course, Jack. Off you go.

(LEWIS exits.)

WARNIE. I would be most grateful for a drink, Joy.

JOY. That's kind of you, Warnie. I must admit, I found that an unusual experience.

WARNIE. Yes. You must forgive Jack.

JOY. Oh, I'm getting to know him a little by now. I think I understand him. I'm very grateful to him.

WARNIE. Nobody is to know, he tells me.

JOY. That's right. Best that way.

WARNIE. What he actually said was, it will be as if it never happened.

JOY. Yes.

WARNIE. Odd business.

JOY. It is that.

WARNIE. Jack plays safe, you see. Always has.

JOY. I do rather need that drink.

(THEY exit. The screen rises to reveal Joy's house. LEWIS is there with DOUGLAS, who is in his pyjamas.)

LEWIS. So how do you like it here?

DOUGLAS. Not much. Mom says we don't have to stay if we don't like it.

LEWIS. So you're seeing if you like it.

DOUGLAS. Except I don't.

LEWIS. What about your mother?

DOUGLAS. I guess she likes it.

LEWIS. And you want to stay with her?

DOUGLAS. Yes. Have you met my dad?

LEWIS. No.

DOUGLAS. He's okay, my dad. But I love mom the best.

JOY. (*Enters.*) Douglas. Bed.

DOUGLAS. (*Turns to go.*) 'Night, Mr. Lewis.

LEWIS. Good night, Douglas.

JOY. One chapter.

(DOUGLAS exits.)

LEWIS. He's so obedient. I like him.

JOY. He likes you.

LEWIS. He doesn't seem very impressed by England.

JOY. He'll get used to it.

LEWIS. So this is it, is it? Land of Hope and Glory?

JOY. I think so. I'm happier here than I've been in a long time.

LEWIS. That's good.

JOY. Mostly because of you, Jack. One good friend can make all the difference.

LEWIS. You're not getting sick of the sight of me?

JOY. Not yet. Though heaven knows what the neighbors think.

LEWIS. The worst, I've no doubt.

JOY. Don't you sometimes burst to share the joke?

LEWIS. What joke?

JOY. Well. Here's the neighbors thinking we're unmarried and up to all sorts of wickedness, while all along we're married and up to nothing at all.

LEWIS. I'd better be on my merry way.

JOY. (*SHE sees that her joke makes him uneasy.*) Only technically married, of course.

LEWIS. Oh, look, do you think I come round too often?

JOY. Too often for what? We're friends. That's what we agreed. Good friends.

(*LEWIS prepares to leave.*
JOY gets his coat and helps him on with it. Her hands rest on his shoulders. HE moves away.)

JOY. I'm not going to talk about it anymore. You get that twitchy look in your eyes, and you start feeling in your coat pockets, like there's something there you have to find.

(*LEWIS is doing just as she describes. HE stops, and removes his hands from his pockets.*)

LEWIS. You know me too well.

JOY. Don't say that. Just say I know you.

LEWIS. You know me.

DOUGLAS. (*Offstage*) Mom! I'm ready!

JOY. I'll be right there.

LEWIS. I'll say good night then. (*As LEWIS leaves, a sudden pain strikes her.*)

JOY. Ah!

LEWIS. What is it?

JOY. It's nothing. I just stumbled. I'm fine. See you soon.

LEWIS. Well, good night then.

JOY. Good night, Jack.

(HE pats her on one arm and THEY exchange a peck on the cheek. LEWIS exits.

JOY stands looking after him. Then SHE turns to go to Douglas. HER body twists, and her mouth opens in a silent scream. Suddenly, SHE crumples to the floor.)

CURTAIN

ACT II

The screen is down. LEWIS enters and speaks to the audience, as he did at the beginning of the play.

As the talk proceeds, there are signs that he is using it to persuade himself of a belief that is beginning to slide. However, at this stage, he hardly realizes this process himself.

LEWIS. Recently a friend of mine, a brave and Christian woman, collapsed in terrible pain. One minute she seemed fit and well. The next minute she was in agony. She is now in hospital, suffering from advanced bone cancer, and almost certainly dying. Why?

I find it hard to believe that God loves her. If you love someone, you don't want them to suffer. You can't bear it. You want to take their suffering onto yourself. If even I feel like that, why doesn't God? Not just once in history, on the cross, but again and again? Today. Now.

It's at times like this that we have to remind ourselves of the very core of the Christian faith. There are other worlds than this. This world, that seems so real, is no more than a shadow of the life to come. If we believe that all is well in this present life, if we can imagine nothing more satisfactory than this present life, then we are under a dangerous illusion. All is not well. Believe me, all is not well.

(His present experience, Joy's suffering, breaks through the familiar pattern of his lecture.)

Suffering ... by suffering ... through suffering, we release our hold on the toys of this world, and know that our true good lies in another world. But after we have suffered so much, must we still suffer more? And more?

(He has no answer to this question, which torments him. All he can do is repeat his familiar lines, wanting to believe them.)

We are like blocks of stone, out of which the sculptor carves the forms of men. The blows of his chisel, which hurt us so much, are what make us perfect. *(HE turns aside, to hide his feelings.)*

(WARNIE enters, with DOUGLAS. HE sits DOUGLAS down on a chair and comes to LEWIS. DOUGLAS reads the book he is carrying.)

WARNIE. How is she?

LEWIS. Not good. Not good.

WARNIE. I'm sorry, Jack.

LEWIS. I want her to be well again, you see.

WARNIE. Of course you do. We all do.

LEWIS. What a dangerous world we live in, Warnie. How full of cutting edges. They give her morphine, you know. No morphine for me.

WARNIE. You've been up all night, Jack. You must get some sleep.

LEWIS. I can't sleep. I've never felt more awake in my life. *(HE moves restlessly about.)*

LEWIS. You see, Warnie, this isn't the right time. It's too soon.

WARNIE. Too soon for what, Jack?

LEWIS. I haven't had time, you see, Warnie.

WARNIE. Time for what, Jack?

LEWIS. Time to talk. Time to get to know her. Time to … say things.

(Now WARNIE understands.)

WARNIE. It doesn't take long.

LEWIS. No. I suppose not.

WARNIE. Whatever it is, I should just say it.

LEWIS. Would you, Warnie? You're quite right, of course. But it's difficult, you see.

WARNIE. Yes. I do see that.

LEWIS. I just want her to be well again. That's all.

(The screen rises, revealing a hospital room. JOY lies in a bed. A NURSE comes forward to collect Douglas. LEWIS goes to Douglas to prepare him.)

LEWIS. Douglas, you know she's not strong, don't you? But she's in very good hands. Very good hands. She sleeps a lot. You mustn't mind that. Sleep's good for her. Sleep, the great healer.

WARNIE. Are you a muffin man, Douglas? Like muffins, do you?

DOUGLAS. Yes.

WARNIE. We'll have a muffin tea later. I shall like that.

(The NURSE takes DOUGLAS to Joy's bedside.)

NURSE. Douglas, you can see your mother now.

LEWIS. Warnie, that's *The Magician's Nephew* he's carrying around with him.

WARNIE. Yes. I noticed.

LEWIS. The boy travels to Narnia, and picks a magic apple, and brings it back to his dying mother, and makes her well again.

WARNIE. Poor kid.

LEWIS. I'm a fraud, Warnie.

(A DOCTOR enters and approaches Lewis.)

DOCTOR. Mr. Lewis.

LEWIS. Ah, Doctor. Any change?

DOCTOR. She's been sleeping. Otherwise, nothing to report, really.

LEWIS. How much has she been told?

DOCTOR. She's been told that the cancer has eaten through her left femur. That she has a malignant tumor in one breast. She knows it's serious. How can she not know? Her hipbone snapped like a frozen twig.

LEWIS. So suddenly. I don't understand. How can this have happened with no warning?

DOCTOR. I'm told there had been occasional pain before.

LEWIS. Everyone has occasional pain.

DOCTOR. That's often how it goes, I'm afraid.

LEWIS. I just don't understand it.

DOCTOR. To tell you the truth, Mr. Lewis, nor do we.

WARNIE. How bad is it?

LEWIS. She's likely to die.

DOCTOR. That's putting it more starkly than I would choose. I don't pretend to be able to prophesy the future.

LEWIS. No. But it's true, isn't it?

DOCTOR. The cancer is very advanced.

(Inside the hospital room, DOUGLAS kisses his mother and leaves her. HE comes out into the corridor.)

LEWIS. Right. Thank you, Doctor.

(The DOCTOR exits. WARNIE takes charge of Douglas.)

WARNIE. Muffins. Muffins. That's what's needed. There's bound to be muffins somewhere.

(WARNIE and DOUGLAS exit.
LEWIS walks on alone into the hospital room, where JOY lies in bed, weakened by pain and by painkillers.)

LEWIS. Hello, Joy.

JOY. Hello, Jack.

LEWIS. How's the pain?

JOY. Kind of pushy.

LEWIS. Don't talk if it hurts.

JOY. Did you visit before?

LEWIS. Yes. A couple of times.

JOY. I thought so.

LEWIS. They're going to operate on the broken hip tomorrow.

JOY. I'm sorry, Jack. I didn't mean you to have all this bother.

LEWIS. Tush, woman. You're the one who's having the bother.

JOY. What I mean is, I don't expect you to worry about me.

LEWIS. Oh? And who do you expect to worry about you?

JOY. You know what I'm trying to say.

LEWIS. Who else should be worrying about you but me? You are my wife.

JOY. Technically.

LEWIS. Then I shall worry about you technically.

JOY. Just how much is there to worry about, Jack? They won't tell me.

LEWIS. That's because they're not sure themselves.

JOY. Tell me, Jack.

LEWIS. I don't know any more than they do, Joy.

JOY. Please.

(Pause.)

LEWIS. They expect you to die.

JOY. Thank you. *(Having got what she wanted, SHE pauses to regain strength. Then.)* What do you say, Jack? I'm a Jew. Divorced. Broke. And I'm dying of cancer. Do I get a discount?

LEWIS. I don't want to lose you, Joy.

JOY. I don't want to be lost. .. You know something? You seem different. You look at me properly now.

LEWIS. Didn't I before?
JOY. Not properly.
LEWIS. Would you give me your hand?

(SHE gives him her hand. HE holds it and strokes it.)

JOY. Can I say anything I want, Jack?
LEWIS. Yes.
JOY. Anything?
LEWIS. Yes.
JOY. You know it anyway.
LEWIS. Yes.
JOY. I'm still going to say it.
LEWIS. You say it.
JOY. I love you, Jack.

(HE seems about to respond with a declaration of his own, but it does not quite come out.)

LEWIS. Better now?
JOY. Better. Do you mind?
LEWIS. No.

(A spasm of pain passes through her.
LEWIS watches JOY in pain. HE can't bear it. HE goes looking for the Nurse.)

LEWIS. Nurse! Nurse!

(The NURSE enters and examines Joy.)

NURSE. I'll fetch the doctor.

(The NURSE leaves. LEWIS holds Joy's hand as SHE
    suffers.
The DOCTOR enters at last and comes to Joy's side. The
    screen falls. LEWIS exits.
HARRINGTON and RILEY enter. THEY stroll across the
    stage together, gravely discussing their friend's
    situation.)

HARRINGTON. Poor Jack. It's knocked him
completely off-balance.
    RILEY. Looks bad, does it?
    HARRINGTON. Oh yes. They don't expect her to live.
    RILEY. Sad business.
    HARRINGTON. Has he said anything to you?
    RILEY. About her?
    HARRINGTON. Yes.
    RILEY. No. Nothing.
    OAKLEY. (*Crosses the stage.*) Morning, Harry.
    HARRINGTON. Morning, Maurice.
    OAKLEY. Christopher.
    RILEY. Maurice.

(OAKLEY exits.)

HARRINGTON. I don't suppose you were listening in
to the wireless last night?
    RILEY. Jack wasn't on, was he?
    HARRINGTON. No, no. It was "Twenty Questions."
You're not a Gilbert Harding appreciator, then?
    RILEY. His fascination has eluded me so far.

HARRINGTON. (*Chuckles at the memory.*) Oh, he's something quite tremendous. The other day he said, "When I hear the words 'ethical' and 'artistic,' I say fiddle-de-dee and tiddly-push."

RILEY. Ye-es. That is rather good.

(LEWIS enters, in a distracted state.)

HARRINGTON. Do you listen to "Twenty Questions," Jack?

LEWIS. "Twenty Questions"? No. I can't say I do, Harry.

RILEY. Other things to think about, eh, Jack.

LEWIS. Other things. Yes.

(There is a short, awkward pause. Neither RILEY nor HARRINGTON feels quite able to bring up the subject of Joy. LEWIS resolves the awkwardness by starting to speak of her, without introduction, as if she is as much in their minds as she is in his.)

LEWIS. She's in very good hands. She sleeps a good deal. Sleep is good, don't you think? Sleep, the great healer.

HARRINGTON. Great healer.

RILEY. I'm so sorry about all this, Jack.

LEWIS. Yes. It's all come too soon, you see. Her affairs aren't in order. What's to happen to Douglas, for example?

HARRINGTON. I suppose his father—

LEWIS. She doesn't want that. He drinks, you see.

HARRINGTON. I don't really see what you can do about that.

LEWIS. Do you think I should take the boy in?

HARRINGTON. There must be relatives, Jack. I mean, it's not as if ...

LEWIS. Not as if what?

HARRINGTON. Well, she's your friend, of course, but she's not ... well, family.

LEWIS. Not my wife?

HARRINGTON. (*Gives a nervous laugh at such a prospect.*) No. Of course not.

LEWIS. Of course not. Impossible. Unthinkable.

HARRINGTON. I only meant—

LEWIS. How could Joy be my wife? I'd have to love her, wouldn't I? I'd have to care more for her than for anyone else in this world. I'd have to be suffering the torments of the damned at the prospect of losing her.

HARRINGTON. (*Awed by Lewis's passionate outburst.*) I'm sorry, Jack. I didn't know.

LEWIS. Nor did I, Harry. (*Suddenly, his manner changes. HE becomes calm, almost businesslike.*) I'm going to marry her, Harry. I've made up my mind. I want you to marry us properly, Harry, before God.

HARRINGTON. (*Now embarrassed professionally as well as personally.*) I think it would be best if we talked about this later, Jack.

LEWIS. We don't have a later.

HARRINGTON. Still. It's not entirely plain sailing, is it? (*HE looks to Riley for support.*)

RILEY. I think Harry's trying to say it's against the rules.

HARRINGTON. She's a divorced woman, Jack. The bishop would never let me.

(LEWIS stares at him as if he understands, but when he speaks it is clear that nothing Harrington has said has gone in.)

LEWIS. I'm going to marry her, Harry. If you won't do it, I'll find someone who will.

HARRINGTON. I don't make the rules.

RILEY. Jack. I can't pretend to understand what's happening to you, but if this is what you want, I wish you both happy.

HARRINGTON. I'm really sorry, Jack.

LEWIS. That's alright, Harry. I understand. *(HE goes toward the hospital room.)*

*(RILEY and HARRINGTON exit as the screen rises.
LEWIS goes back to Joy's bedside. The DOCTOR has left by now.)*

LEWIS. It's me again.

JOY. Did you go?

LEWIS. I went. And I came back.

JOY. This dope they give me. I get confused.

LEWIS. Does it help the pain?

JOY. Oh, yes. It's the strangest sensation. Like the pain's still going on down there, but it's nothing to do with me.

LEWIS. Is your mind clear now?

JOY. How would I know? Try me.

LEWIS. What's fifty-eight take away forty-one?

JOY. (*Wrestles with the sum.*) Seventeen?

LEWIS. That's how old I was when you were born.

JOY. I was a baby. You were almost a man. For a while back there, I thought I might just catch you up. But here I am, back to being a baby again. (*This long speech wears her out, and SHE closes her eyes.*)

LEWIS. (*Looks lovingly down at her.*) Joy?

JOY. Still here.

LEWIS. I'm going to marry you, Joy. I'm going to marry you before God and the world.

JOY. You don't have to, Jack.

LEWIS. I want to. It's what I want.

JOY. Make an honest woman of me.

LEWIS. Not you, Joy. I'm the one who hasn't been honest. Look what it takes to make me see sense.

JOY. Think I overdid it?

LEWIS. Don't leave me, Joy.

JOY. (*SHE smiles. The morphine makes her sleepy. For a moment SHE closes her eyes.*) Back home, we have a quaint old custom. When the guy has made up his mind he wants to marry the girl, he asks her. It's called proposing.

LEWIS. It's the same here.

JOY. Did I miss it?

LEWIS. (*Takes her hand and kisses it.*) Will you marry this foolish, frightened, old man, who needs you more than he can bear to say, and loves you even though he hardly knows how?

JOY. Okay. Just this once.

(*DOUGLAS enters. HE stands in silence, watching.*

WARNIE enters, accompanied by a young PRIEST, who carries a service book. The PRIEST goes to the bedside and opens his book.

LEWIS holds Joy's hand.

JOY is fully awake now, and though weak, radiantly happy. SHE speaks the marriage vows clearly and steadily.)

JOY. I, Joy, take thee, Jack ...

PRIEST. "... to have and to hold, from this day forward ..."

(Behind them, the LIGHTS come up in the Other World space, and the wardrobe door swings open of its own accord. Only DOUGLAS sees this. HE turns and stares.)

JOY. ... to have and to hold, from this day forward...

PRIEST. "... for better, for worse ..."

JOY. ... for better, for worse ...

(DOUGLAS moves softly away from the group toward the Other World space as the familiar ritual continues.)

PRIEST. "... for richer, for poorer ..."

JOY . . . for richer, for poorer . . .

PRIEST. "... in sickness and in health ..."

JOY. ... in sickness and in health ...

PRIEST. "... to love, cherish, and obey ..."

JOY. ... to love, cherish, and obey ...

PRIEST. "... till death us do part."

JOY. ... till death us do part.

*(DOUGLAS has now entered the Other World space. HE
    holds up his hand to a tree that grows there and picks
    from it a glowing magic apple.*
*WARNIE steps forward and gives LEWIS a ring. LEWIS
    puts the ring on Joy's finger.)*

PRIEST. "With this ring I thee wed."
LEWIS. With this ring I thee wed.
PRIEST. "With my body I thee worship."
LEWIS. With my body I thee worship.
PRIEST. "With all my worldly goods I thee endow."
LEWIS. With all my worldly goods I thee endow.

*(DOUGLAS carries the magic apple back into the hospital
    room and kneels at the foot of Joy's bed.)*

PRIEST. "In the name of the Father …
LEWIS. In the name of the Father …
PRIEST. "…and of the Son…"
LEWIS. … and of the Son …
PRIEST. "… and of the Holy Ghost."
LEWIS. … and of the Holy Ghost.
PRIEST. "Amen."
LEWIS. Amen.
PRIEST. Those whom God hath joined together, let no
man put asunder. For as much as Jack and Joy have
consented together in Holy Wedlock and have made witness
of the same before God and this company, I pronounce that
they be Man and Wife together. In the name of the Father
and of the Son and of the Holy Ghost. Amen.

(JOY is now asleep again.

WARNIE and the PRIEST exit. LEWIS kisses Joy's forehead and exits. As he exits, DOUGLAS places the magic apple in his mother's hands. Then HE bends over her and kisses her.

The LIGHT fades on the Other World as the screen falls and DOUGLAS exits.

The DOCTOR enters and goes to Lewis. Time has passed.)

DOCTOR. Well, Mr. Lewis, I think I'm in no danger of overstating the case if I say no news is good news. Given the seriousness of her condition, we have reason to be cautiously optimistic.

LEWIS. I'm sorry, Doctor, but I don't understand a word you're saying. It would help me if you would use words I'm familiar with, like "getting better," "getting worse." "Dying."

DOCTOR. I'm afraid none of those words meet the case. What seems to be happening is that the rate of spread of the disease is slowing down.

LEWIS. You mean she's getting better?

DOCTOR. She's not worse.

LEWIS. Is not being worse better than being worse?

DOCTOR. Put like that, yes.

LEWIS. Then she's getting better, isn't she?

DOCTOR. Mr. Lewis. You're looking at a train standing in a station. It may not be moving right now, but trains move. That's how trains are.

LEWIS. What would be a good sign? People do recover from cancer. It has been known.

DOCTOR. Any sign of returning strength. Any sign that the body is rebuilding the diseased bone.

LEWIS. Did you expect her to make it this far?

DOCTOR. You didn't expect her to make it this far, did you?

LEWIS. (*Accepts this as the Doctor's attempt at encouragement.*) Thank you, Doctor.

(The DOCTOR exits.

LEWIS re-enters the hospital room, where JOY is now sitting up in bed. HE pulls a chair to her bedside and sits down by her. JOY is still weak but in very good spirits.)

LEWIS. I should have brought you something, shouldn't I? Flowers. Grapes. Why grapes, I wonder?

NURSE. Only five minutes, Mr. Lewis.

JOY. Just bring me books, Jack. I'm going crazy here. The nurse has been telling me all about her love life. She's been dating this guy for two years. Will he marry her? How far should she let him go without them being at least engaged? I'm telling you, I was sick with excitement. But she doesn't see him again till Saturday, so I need books.

LEWIS. (*Smiles at her ready chatter. Just looking at her makes him feel happy.*) It strikes me you're rather better.

JOY. Shh! We have to pretend we haven't noticed, or He'll take it away.

LEWIS. So what advice did you give the nurse?

JOY. I said, give him enough to make him want the rest, then nothing till he pays up.

LEWIS. Poor fellow. He hasn't a chance.

JOY. (*Holds up her hand to look at her wedding ring.*) Jack. If I get better, do I have to give the ring back?

LEWIS. No, that's yours forever, Joy. For all eternity.

JOY. You don't have to feel sorry for me now.

LEWIS. Nor for myself. I just want some time with you, Joy.

JOY. Shh! *(SHE glances upward, at God, who mustn't hear.)* Speaking of Him, how did you square it?

LEWIS. Marrying you?

JOY. Yes. You're not the sort to say it's wrong, but I want it anyway.

LEWIS. I did think about it, yes. The argument I gave myself went like this. I want to marry Joy, but if she's married to someone else, I can't. Whatever a divorce court decrees, marriage is indissoluble in the eyes of God. But you see, your husband had been married before. If marriage is indissoluble, he's still married to his first wife. If he's still married to his first wife, he can't have married you. Not in the eyes of God. He wasn't free. So you were never really married to him in the first place.

(JOY laughs.)

LEWIS. Am I being too clever?

JOY. I think you have one of the great minds of the century.

LEWIS. Well, I know that.

NURSE. *(Enters, with screens to put around the bed.)* I said five minutes, Mr. Lewis.

(LEWIS kisses JOY and turns to leave, saying to the Nurse as he goes.)

LEWIS. Good luck on Saturday. *(LEWIS exits as the screen falls.)*

(WARNIE and HARRINGTON enter.)

HARRINGTON. Frankly, I'm worried about him. His behavior is entirely out of character.

WARNIE. It's been a very great shock to him.

HARRINGTON. That's my point. I know they've become good friends—

WARNIE. Husband and wife.

HARRINGTON. Well, quite. I mean, what can one say? The woman is dying.

WARNIE. Not anymore.

HARRINGTON. Not dying?

WARNIE. Jack says she's recovering. The cancer has stopped spreading.

HARRINGTON. *(Disconcerted by this information.)* That's very good news. Excellent news. So what will you do, Warnie?

WARNIE. What do you mean?

HARRINGTON. Well, if she makes a full recovery. Where will you live?

WARNIE. I don t know.

(This point had not occurred to him. It does now.
RILEY enters. HARRINGTON turns to him, expecting to find an ally.)

HARRINGTON. Christopher. Excellent news. Mrs. Gresham is not to die after all.

RILEY. That is good news. *(HE says no more than this, but it is clear he feels deeply relieved.)*

WARNIE. I think we must call her Mrs. Lewis, you know.

HARRINGTON. If she does recover, we shall chalk it up as a victory for the power of prayer.

RILEY. I've never quite understood about prayer. Does God intervene in the world only when asked?

HARRINGTON. It has been known.

RILEY. And what are the qualifications for divine aid? Merit? Intense suffering? Persistent prayer? I mean, how does He choose?

HARRINGTON. I hardly think this is the time or the place for a theological argument.

RILEY. And if God knows what's best for us anyway, why do we need to ask? Doesn't He know already?

LEWIS. (*Enters.*) Doesn't who know what?

HARRINGTON. Jack. Thank goodness. Christopher's being Christopherish about prayer.

LEWIS. Prayer? I pray all the time these days. If I stopped praying, I think I'd stop living.

HARRINGTON. And God hears your prayer, doesn't he? We hear Joy's getting better.

LEWIS. Yes. She is.

HARRINGTON. I m very glad, Jack.

LEWIS. That's not why I pray, Harry. I pray because I can't help myself. I pray because I'm helpless. I pray because the need flows out of me all the time, waking and sleeping. It doesn't change God. It changes me.

RILEY. Now, that I can understand. That's the first sensible thing I've heard anyone say on the subject.

LEWIS. She's getting better, you see. It's quite something. We mustn't expect too much, of course. Mustn't get our hopes up. Shall we go, Warnie?

WARNIE. Ready when you are, Jack.

(HARRINGTON and RILEY exit.
The screen rises to reveal the hospital room again. Joy's
bed is behind the hospital screens.
LEWIS and WARNIE cross to the corridor outside the
hospital room.
The DOCTOR enters. LEWIS turns to him eagerly.)

LEWIS. Well, Doctor?
DOCTOR. I think you should come and see for
yourself.
LEWIS. See what?
DOCTOR. She's doing rather well, all things
considered.

(LEWIS follows the DOCTOR to the screened bed.
WARNIE stays back, not wanting to intrude.
LEWIS stands before the closed screens as the DOCTOR
draws them back.
The bed is empty.
JOY stands beside the bed, supported by crutches and
attended by the watchful NURSE.)

LEWIS. Rather well!
JOY. Hello, Jack. Warnie.
LEWIS. Look at you! Come on now. Show us.

(SHE walks a few cautious steps. WARNIE, the
DOCTOR, and the NURSE clap. LEWIS turns to them
like a proud parent.)

LEWIS. Did you see that, Warnie? Did you?

WARNIE. Good show, Joy. Good show.

LEWIS. Do some more.

DOCTOR. Slowly now.

LEWIS. Of course, of course. That's enough. Rest.

*(The NURSE helps JOY to the side of the bed.
LEWIS goes to the Doctor.)*

LEWIS. When can I take her home?

DOCTOR. As soon as you like. I see no reason to keep her in hospital, so long as the remission continues.

LEWIS. Which is how long?

(The DOCTOR glances toward Joy.)

LEWIS. You can speak openly. She does have an interest in the matter.

DOCTOR. It could be weeks. It could be months.

LEWIS. Why not years?

DOCTOR. In such an advanced case, that would be ... unusual. I'm sorry. You did want to know.

LEWIS. Right. We take what we can get. *(HE goes to Joy.)* How would you like to come home?

JOY. Where's home, Jack?

LEWIS. My house. Our house. You're my wife, remember? Warnie and I are going to look after you.

JOY. Have you asked Warnie?

LEWIS. Ah. *(HE goes over to Warnie.)* Ah, Warnie ...

WARNIE. Don't worry about me, Jack. I'll sort myself out.

LEWIS. Sort yourself out? What do you mean?

WARNIE. New digs. No problem.

LEWIS. Do you want to?

WARNIE. As you wish, Jack.

LEWIS. I don't.

WARNIE. Right you are.

LEWIS. That's settled, then.

WARNIE. *(Kisses Joy.)* See you at home, Joy. *(HE exits.)*

(JOY stands. LEWIS takes her suitcase. THEY walk downstage with the NURSE as the screen comes down behind them.)

JOY. Thank you for everything, Mrs. Braddock.

LEWIS. Yes. Thank you for everything.

JOY. Not bad?

LEWIS. Not bad. *(Pause.)* Now, I don't want to hear any talk of miracles.

JOY. Why not? It's a miracle to me.

LEWIS. Miracles frighten me.

JOY. Take it when it's offered, I say.

LEWIS. I'm frightened of loving God too much for giving you back to me. That way, I could just as easily hate God, later.

JOY. Don't be so hard on yourself, Jack. Thank God now, and let later come later.

LEWIS. Anyway, it's not such a big miracle, really. You coming back to life.

JOY. What's wrong with it? You leave my miracle alone.

LEWIS. You were alive before. I wasn't.

JOY. What are you talking about?

LEWIS. I started living when I started loving you, Joy. That makes me only a few months old.

JOY. Could be a short life, Jack.

LEWIS. At least it's a life.

(The screen rises to reveal the study at The Kilns. THEY enter.)

LEWIS. Welcome home!

JOY. It really does feel like home.

LEWIS. Oh, does it? I am pleased.

JOY. Jack. I have a question I've never dared ask before. But now that we're married ...

LEWIS. Anything, Joy.

JOY. Do you ever turn the heat on in here?

LEWIS. I'm afraid it's broken.

JOY. When did it stop working?

LEWIS. Good heavens, I can't remember. Ten years ago? Put your coat on, I always do.

JOY. This world is not a perfect place, Jack. And your house is less perfect than most of it. Will you let me purge it a little?

LEWIS. It's your home now, Joy. Purge away.

JOY. *(Hits a chair with her cane. Dust rises.)* Look at that. *(SHE turns to him and strokes his shoulder.)* And how about you? I'm not caressing you lovingly, I'm removing the dust. Actually, I am caressing you lovingly.

(THEY look into each other's eyes. THEY embrace and kiss.

LEWIS then helps her into her chair, brings a footstool for
her legs, and covers her with an afghan. HE then brings
her a crossword puzzle and a pen.)

JOY. Such service. I should get sick more often.

(LEWIS exits, carrying one of her canes away.
WARNIE enters, reading a newspaper, and settles down in
his usual chair.
DOUGLAS enters, carrying a chess board set up with chess
pieces, which HE sets beside WARNIE'S chair. HE
ponders the game.
WARNIE reads aloud from his newspaper.)

WARNIE. "The Queen has announced that the Royal
Family's surname will be changed to Mountbatten-
Windsor."

JOY. *(Studying the crossword.)* "Quintessence,
botanically expressed." Four.

WARNIE. Used to be something foreign. Then it
became Windsor. Pith.

JOY. Pith.

WARNIE. "The new surname will not apply until
Prince Charles has grandsons." How very strange.

(WARNIE makes a move in the chess game. LEWIS has
re-entered and stands behind Douglas, watching the
game.)

DOUGLAS. Oh no! I didn't see that! Can't I have my
move again?

LEWIS. You don't need to. Look. Check.

DOUGLAS. Oh yes.

JOY. Jack, make him work it out for himself. It's the only way he'll learn.

LEWIS. Is that so, Joy? Maybe we should send him to the University of Hard Knocks. He could learn to say, "I don't know much about art, but I call a spade a spade."

JOY. I knew it! That Honest Jack act you pull on your radio talks, it's all a front. You're an intellectual snob.

LEWIS. Oh, really? And am I a "highbrow," and a "smug academic"?

JOY. I'm not insulting you, Jack. I'm criticizing you.

LEWIS. I see. Please enlighten me.

JOY. The educational system in this country is prehistoric. The boys at Douglas's school talk about going to a university like it was going to the moon.

LEWIS. How is that a criticism of me? I'd like as many boys to go to university as possible.

JOY. I count three buried assumptions there. "I'd like"—that's the language of mild preference, not active concern. You don't say "I'd like as many boys to be saved from starvation as possible."

LEWIS. My language reflects—

JOY. Wait. I haven't finished. Second buried assumption. "Boys." What about girls?

LEWIS. Conceded. Go on.

JOY. Third buried assumption. You'd like as many to go to university "as possible." What makes it possible, Jack? God? Chance? The weather? How about people like you? The high priests of the sacred cult of the intellectual elite?

LEWIS. Verbal raspberries.

JOY. You always want the last word.

LEWIS. Precious hope of that.

WARNIE. Honeymoon.

JOY. What?

LEWIS. What was that, Warnie?

WARNIE. Marriage. Honeymoon. That's the way of it.
You should have a honeymoon.

LEWIS. Joy's not up to traveling.

JOY. I suppose this is our honeymoon, Warnie.

LEWIS. I suppose it is.

JOY. So how come we're carrying on as if we've been
married for years?

LEWIS. Is that what we're doing?

JOY. You are an intellectual bully, you know.

LEWIS. That makes two of us. I think I'm too old to
change now. Do you mind?

JOY. You being too old or you being a bully?

LEWIS. Either.

JOY. No. I don't mind. Do you mind?

LEWIS. No. I don't want to be young anymore. When
you're young, you're always looking ahead, always waiting
for something better to come round the next bend in the
road. I'm not looking ahead anymore. I'm with you, here,
now, and that's enough.

JOY. People go on journeys for their honeymoon, Jack.

LEWIS. What, you mean abroad?

JOY. No need to sound so alarmed.

LEWIS. My mother took Warnie and me to Berneval,
near Dieppe, the summer before she died. My one and only
holiday abroad.

WARNIE. Nineteen hundred and seven.

LEWIS. Where do you want to go?

JOY. I've always wanted to go to Greece. To see the Parthenon. And the temple of Apollo at Delphi. And the lion gates of Mycenae.

LEWIS. Where would we stay?

JOY. Some little Greek hotel.

LEWIS. Are you up to it?

JOY. Me? If you are.

LEWIS. I truly believe that if I had to go into an hotel with a woman, and sign the register, I'd blush.

WARNIE. That's settled, then.

JOY. (*Quotes Byron, in declamatory style.*) The isles of Greece. The isles of Greece.

(*As JOY and LEWIS move downstage, the screen falls behind them. LEWIS picks up her quotation and continues it with her.*)

JOY and LEWIS.
    Where burning Sappho loved and sung
    Where grew the arts of war and peace
    Where Delos rose and Phoebus sprung
    Eternal summer gilds them yet
    But all except their sun is set.

JOY. And there it is as advertised, not yet set. I love the sun. Don't you love the sun?

LEWIS. Dreadful glare, isn't there?

(*A WAITER has entered with their luggage.*)

LEWIS. I never feel at ease in hotels. There's always someone hanging around trying to be helpful.

JOY. Well, I like them. And I especially like room service.

LEWIS. Room service? I always used to believe that room service was saying prayers in bed.

JOY. Well, you order some prayers if you want. Me, I want a gin and tonic.

LEWIS. Now? You only just had breakfast.

JOY. So?

LEWIS. *(To Waiter.)* Alright. I'd like to order some drinks if we may, to be brought up to our room, if that's convenient. We'd like a gin and tonic, and—*(HE pauses, not sure what he wants for himself.)*—and a gin and tonic. So that's two gin and tonics ... actually, two gins and tonic, to be strictly accurate.

(The WAITER leaves.)

JOY. You don't drink gin.

LEWIS. Yes, I know. I'm afraid I panicked.

JOY. I love the sun. People used to worship the sun. I can understand it.

LEWIS. I can understand people who worship the sun in England, where the sun is invisible. But here—look at it, hanging around like a waiter hoping for a tip. No class. No mystery.

JOY. No, Jack. It's a feeling. You just don't know how to be in the sun.

LEWIS. What do you mean?

JOY. Come here and I'll show you.

LEWIS. You know I don't like surprises.

JOY. Come over here.

LEWIS. This isn't going to work.

JOY. Now put that face of yours up here. Feel it on your face. The sun so close you could stick out your tongue and lick it. No words. No thoughts. Just the sun on your face. The sound of the wind in the olive trees. In this land nothing is impossible. Nothing is forbidden. You could even take off your coat.

(The WAITER enters with drinks as JOY has her arms around Lewis, embracing him inside his jacket.)

LEWIS. Look out, there's somebody there. *(To Waiter.)* Sorry about that. *(LEWIS hands JOY a drink.)* You all right?

JOY. I'm fine. I'm great.

(LEWIS hands drinks back to WAITER.
The screen rises. LEWIS and JOY turn and head into the garden at The Kilns.)

JOY. I am so happy. I don't think I've ever been so happy in my life.

LEWIS. Nor I. Not since the day I was elected a fellow of Magdalen.

JOY. No kidding! I didn't think there was any experience to beat that this side of Paradise.

LEWIS. This is paradise for me. Now.

JOY. Don't say that, Jack. Paradise lasts, I hope. It's beautiful here. Being with you is everything I want. But it's not going to last.

LEWIS. We don't need to think of that now. I don't want to spoil the time we have together.

JOY. It doesn't spoil it. It makes it precious. The small things. The ordinary things. Each time you touch me, I feel it like a shock. Your nearness. Your reality. You. *(SHE looks at him, forcing him to face what is coming.)* What will you do when I die?

LEWIS. I don't know.

JOY. I want to be with you then, Jack. The only way I can do that is to talk to you about it now.

LEWIS. I shall manage. Don't worry about me.

JOY. I think it can be better than that. Better than just managing. What I'm trying to say is that pain, then, is part of this happiness, now. That's the deal.

(Through the sequences of speeches that follow, the LIGHTS change, moving through evening to night. LEWIS and JOY speak in a reflective, almost incantatory way. Time and memories are passing)

LEWIS. We'll have no clocks. No calendars. No clocks.

JOY. I know your footsteps. I can tell it's you, long before you reach the house. I know it's you coming up the road.

LEWIS. I never thought I could be so happy, so late in life. Every day when I come home, there you are.

JOY. The first words you speak, I know what kind of a mood you're in. Just from the sound of your voice. I watch you when you're working at your desk. I study you. I learn you.

LEWIS. Every day when I come home, there you are. I can't get used to that. Every day it surprises me. There you are. It's the sheer availability of the happiness that takes my breath away. I reach out, and there you are. I hold you in my arms. I kiss you. All I have to do is reach out, and there you are. You've made the world kind to me, and I'm so grateful. Grateful for all the ordinary domestic pleasures.

(The pain returns to Joy. SHE feels it but tries not to show it.)

LEWIS. I think I love you too much, Joy. I can't bear to see you in pain.

JOY. The pain doesn't matter. It keeps me quiet.

LEWIS. When it gets close, you find out whether you believe or not.

JOY. Only shadows, Jack. That's what you're always saying. Real life hasn't begun yet. You'd just better be right. *(SHE slips into an exhausted sleep.)*

(DOUGLAS enters.)

LEWIS. Ah, Douglas. Your mother's very sick, I'm afraid.

DOUGLAS. She's going to die, isn't she?

(LEWIS doesn't know how to respond.)

DOUGLAS. Why?
LEWIS. I don't know.
DOUGLAS. Can't you do something?
LEWIS. I'm afraid not.
DOUGLAS. Okay. *(HE exits.)*

(LEWIS draws a chair up beside Joy and sits down. For a
    few moments HE watches her. Then HE drifts into a
    half-sleep, exhausted himself.
The LIGHTING changes slowly, to night-time.
JOY opens her eyes. SHE is very weak.)

JOY. Still here?

LEWIS. (*Wakes.*) Still here.

JOY. Go to bed. Get some sleep.

LEWIS. Soon.

JOY. Jack. Has it been worth it?

LEWIS. Three years of happiness?

JOY. Tell me you'll be alright.

LEWIS. I'll be alright.

JOY. Can we talk about it?

LEWIS. We've never pretended with each other.

JOY. No. Never pretended.

LEWIS. Are you afraid?

JOY. Of dying?

LEWIS. Yes.

JOY. I'm tired, Jack. I want to rest. I just don't want to leave you.

LEWIS. I don't want you to go.

JOY. Too much pain.

LEWIS. I know.

JOY. Other worlds. It has to be more than we can imagine. Even more than you can imagine.

LEWIS. Far more.

JOY. I love your other worlds, Jack. That was how I first fell in love with you. Long before I met you.

LEWIS. Just stories, Joy.

JOY. Magical stories.

LEWIS. I don't know what to do, Joy. You'll have to tell me what to do.

JOY. You have to let me go, Jack.

LEWIS. I'm not sure that I can.

(A silence. JOY is in too much pain to speak. Then the thought of her son breaks through, bringing another sort of pain.)

JOY. Douglas—will you take care of—

LEWIS. Of course I will, Joy.

JOY. He pretends not to mind.

LEWIS. I know.

JOY. Like you.

LEWIS. No pretending anymore.

JOY. I've loved you so much, Jack.

(LEWIS takes her hand and presses it to his lips, trying not to show his own pain.)

JOY. It's always easier for the one who goes first.

(LEWIS can see that the effort of talking is too much for her.)

LEWIS. Don't talk anymore. You rest.

(SHE nods her head and closes her eyes
By now all we can see are the two of them, deep in the night.
LEWIS sits with his chin resting in his hands, speaking softly into the darkness.)

LEWIS. Not much more to say. I love you, Joy. I love you so much. You've made me so happy. I didn't know I could be so happy. You're the truest person I've ever known. Sweet Jesus, be with my beloved wife, Joy. Forgive me if I love her too much. Have mercy on us both.

JOY. (*HER eyes open. SHE speaks very faintly.*) Get some sleep, Jack.

LEWIS. How's the pain?

JOY. Not too good. Only shadows.

LEWIS. Only shadows.

(HER eyes close again. LEWIS rises, stoops and kisses her, and walks softly out of the pool of light.

The LIGHT on JOY fades slowly to black as the screen comes in.)

HARRINGTON. Naturally I wouldn't say this to Jack, but better sooner than later. Better quick than slow. After all, there was no question about it. The writing was on the wall.

GREGG. Is he taking it very hard?

HARRINGTON. He's a remarkable man, Jack. Faith solid as a rock.

RILEY. Harry, those few well-chosen words at the church—did I hear you correctly? It seemed to me that you said something like "All who knew her loved her."

HARRINGTON. Something like that.

RILEY. Not quite God's own truth, was it?

HARRINGTON. Good grief, Christopher, what was I supposed to say? That nobody could stand her?

RILEY. Jack loved her. That's what's true, and that's what matters. But I didn't and you didn't.

HARRINGTON. She is dead.

RILEY. Death does not improve the character.

(The screen goes up and THEY join WARNIE and GREGG, who are seated at the college high table.)

GREGG. You don't love anyone, Christopher, as far as I can see.

RILEY. That may well be true, but Harry still shouldn't tell whoppers.

HARRINGTON. Jack was standing six feet away.

RILEY. Jack wouldn't have minded. He's changed. She did that. She was a remarkable woman. But I'm damned if I'm going to start liking her just because she's dead.

HARRINGTON. Did you like her, Warnie?

WARNIE. Not at first. But oh, yes.

(LEWIS enters. An awkward silence falls as he comes to his place at table.)

LEWIS. I wasn't going to come. Then I thought I would. *(HE sits. HE sounds perfectly calm.)*

HARRINGTON. Life must go on.

LEWIS. I don't know that it must. But it certainly does.

GREGG. I'm sorry I wasn't able to be at the church.

LEWIS. Not important, Alan.

HARRINGTON. My little address, Jack. Was it …?

LEWIS. Please forgive me, Harry. I haven't the slightest idea what you said in church. I didn't hear a word.

HARRINGTON. Fine. Fine. Perfectly understandable.

RILEY. Are you alright, Jack?

LEWIS. No.

HARRINGTON. Thank God for your faith, Jack. Where would you be without that?

LEWIS. I'd be here, drinking my port.

HARRINGTON. What I mean to say, Jack, is that it's only faith that makes any sense of times like this.

LEWIS. (*Puts down his glass*.) No, I'm sorry, Harry, but it won't do. This is a mess, and that's all there is to it.

HARRINGTON. A mess?

LEWIS. What sense do you make of it? You tell me.

HARRINGTON. But, Jack—we have to have faith that God knows—

LEWIS. God knows. Yes, God knows. I don't doubt that. God knows. But does God care? Did He care about Joy?

HARRINGTON. Why are you talking like this, Jack? We can't see what's best for us. You know that. We're not the Creator.

LEWIS. No. We're the creatures. We're the rats in the cosmic laboratory. I've no doubt the great experiment is for our own good, eventually, but that still makes God the vivisectionist.

HARRINGTON. This is your grief talking.

LEWIS. What was talking before? My complacency?

HARRINGTON. Please, Jack. Please.

LEWIS. I'm sorry, Harry. You're a good man. I don't mean to distress you. But the fact is, I've come up against a bit of experience recently. Experience is a brutal teacher, but you learn fast. I'm sorry. I shouldn't have come this

evening. I'm not fit company. *(HE rises.)* If you'll forgive
me. *(HE leaves the table.)*
    WARNIE. Excuse me.

*(WARNIE follows LEWIS to where HE stands, frowning,
    by himself. The screen falls.)*

    LEWIS. Sorry about that, Warnie. Not necessary.
    WARNIE. Everybody understands, Jack.
    LEWIS. I can't see her anymore. I can't remember her
face. What's happening to me?
    WARNIE. I expect it's shock.
    LEWIS. I'm so terribly afraid. Of never seeing her
again. Of thinking that suffering is just suffering after all.
No cause. No purpose. No pattern. No sense. Just pain, in
a world of pain.
    WARNIE. I don't know what to tell you, Jack.
    LEWIS. Nothing. There's nothing to say.

(THEY are silent for a few moments.
*DOUGLAS enters on the far side of the stage. HE is
    profoundly hurt by his mother's death but is refusing to
    show it.)*

    WARNIE. Jack.
    LEWIS. Yes.
    WARNIE. About Douglas.
    LEWIS. Yes.
    WARNIE. Your grief is your business. Maybe you feel
life is a mess. Maybe it is. But he's only a child.
    LEWIS. What am I supposed to do about it?
    WARNIE. Talk to him.

LEWIS. I don't know what to say to him.

WARNIE. Just talk to him. (*WARNIE exits.*)

LEWIS. (*Walks across to Douglas. HE speaks to the boy in a matter-of-fact way, as if they are equals.*) When I was your age, my mother died. That was cancer too. I thought that if I prayed for her to get better, and if I really believed she'd get better, then she wouldn't die. But she did.

DOUGLAS. It doesn't work.

LEWIS. No. It doesn't work.

DOUGLAS. I don't care.

LEWIS. I do. When I'm alone, I start crying. Do you cry?

DOUGLAS. No.

LEWIS. I didn't when I was your age. (*A brief pause.*) I loved your mother very much.

DOUGLAS. That's okay.

LEWIS. I loved her too much. She knew that. She said to me, "Is it worth it?" She knew how it would be later. (*Pause.*) It doesn't seem fair, does it? If you want the love, you have to have the pain.

DOUGLAS. I don't see why she had to get sick.

LEWIS. Nor I. (*Pause.*) You can't hold on to things. You have to let them go.

DOUGLAS. Jack?

LEWIS. Yes.

DOUGLAS. Do you believe in heaven?

LEWIS. Yes.

DOUGLAS. I don't believe in heaven.

LEWIS. That's okay.

DOUGLAS. I sure would like to see her again.

LEWIS. Me too.

(DOUGLAS can't take any more. HE reaches out for comfort, pressing himself against Lewis. LEWIS wraps his arms around the boy, and at last his own tears break through, in heartbreaking sobs, unloosing the grief of a lifetime. His emotion releases the tears that have been waiting in the boy.
As THEY fall quiet, DOUGLAS detaches himself and exits.
LEWIS turns to face the audience and begins to speak quietly. His words are a version of the talk he has given earlier, now transformed by his own suffering.)

LEWIS. We are like blocks of stone, out of which the sculptor carves the forms of men. The blows of his chisel, which hurt us so much, are what make us perfect.

No shadows here. Only darkness, and silence, and the pain that cries like a child.

It ends, like all affairs of the heart, with exhaustion. Only so much pain is possible. Then, rest.

So it comes about that, when I am quiet, when I am quiet, she returns to me. There she is, in my mind, in my memory, coming towards me, and I love her again as I did before, even though I know I will lose her again, and be hurt again.

So you can say if you like that Jack Lewis has no answer to the question after all, except this: I have been given the choice twice in my life. The boy chose safety. The man chooses suffering.

(HE now speaks to her, in his memory.)

LEWIS. I went to my wardrobe this morning. I was looking for my old brown jacket, the one I used to wear before—I'd forgotten that you'd carried out one of your purges there. Just before we went to Greece, I think it was. I find I can live with the pain, after all. The pain, now, is part of the happiness, then. That's the deal.

Only shadows, Joy.

Final Curtain

FURNITURE AND PROPERTY LIST
ACT I

On stage:
　　Outer Area
　　Tree with magic apples
　　Books on bookshelves

　　Inner Area
　　Large high-table. *On it:* silver table settings, glasses, decanter of port, etc.
　　Beneath it: scarves and hats for Warnie and Lewis
　　Six chairs

Personal:
　　Lewis: wrist-watch (worn throughout), newspaper
　　Warnie: wrist-watch (worn throughout)

　　When the screen in place
　　Inner Area
Strike:
　　High-table and six chairs
Set:
　　Desk. *On it:* pens, papers, books, etc.
　　Chair
　　Armchair
　　Small table

Off stage:
　　Bicycle (Gregg) Tray of breakfast items, letters (including airmail letter), newspaper (Warnie)

When screen in place
    Inner Area
Strike:
    Breakfast items, tray, newspaper, letters

    Outer Area
Set:
    Tea table and four chairs DL. *On table:* bell

Off stage:
    Hardback edition of *The Magician's Nephew*
    (Douglas)
    Tray of tea items (Waiter)

The screen rises
    Outer Area
Strike:
    Tea table and four chairs

Off stage:
    Paperchains (Warnie)
    Tray of tea items, including glass of squash and cake
      (Lewis)
    Glasses (Warnie, Riley, Oakley and Harrington)
    Breakfast tray, newspaper (Warnie)
    Letters (Lewis)
    Typescript (Riley)

Personal:
    Lewis: money, fountain pen
    Waiter: note-pad, pencil
    Joy: airmail letter

When screen in place
  Inner Area
Strike:
  All items
Set:
  Packing cases containing books and various items
    wrapped in newspaper
  Bookshelves

When screen in place
  Inner Area
Strike:
  Items
Set:
  Table. *On it:* pen, register, service book

Off stage:
  Deckchair, book (Warnie)
  Deckchair, book (Lewis)
  Pile of books (Lewis)

When screen in place
  Inner Area
Strike:
  All items
Set:
  Armchair and Lewis's coat

ACT II

  Outer Area
Set:

Chair DR

Inner Area
Hospital bed with bedclothes and pillows
Chair

Off stage:
    Book (Douglas)

When screen in place
    Outer Area
Strike:
    Chair DR

Off stage:
    Service book (Priest)
    Hospital screens (Nurse)

Personal:
    Warnie: wedding ring in pocket

When screen in place
    Inner Area
Set:
    Crutches and coat for Joy
Re-set:
    Hospital screens around bed

When screen in place
    Inner Area
Strike:
    All items

Set:
  Desk. *On it:* pens, papers, books, etc.
  Chair
  Armchair
  Small table
  Chair

Off stage:
  Newspaper (Warnie)
  Chessboard and pieces (Douglas)

When screen in place
  Inner Area
Strike:
  All items
Set:
  Sofa
  Telephone

During Black-out
  Inner Area
Strike: All items
Set:
  High-table. *On it;* silver table settings, glasses,
    decanter of port, etc.
  Six chairs

FURNITURE AND PROPERTY LIST

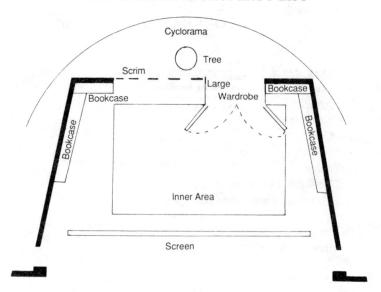

ACT I

On stage: Outer Area
Tree with magic apples
Books on bookshelves

Inner Area
Large high-table. *On it*: silver table settings, glasses, decanter of port, etc.
Beneath it: scarves and hats for **Warnie** and **Lewis**
Six chairs

Personal: **Lewis**: wrist-watch (worn throughout), newspaper
Warnie: wrist-watch (worn throughout)

When the screen in place (page 4)
Inner Area
Strike: High-table and six chairs

Set: Desk. *On it*: pens, papers, books, etc.
Chair
Armchair
Small table

Off stage: Bicycle (**Gregg**)
Tray of breakfast items, letters (including airmail letter), newspaper (**Warnie**)

THE FILM SOCIETY
Jon Robin Baitz
(Little Theatre) Dramatic comedy
4m., 2f. Various ints. (may be unit set)

Imagine the best of Simon Gray crossed with the best of Athol Fugard. The New York critics lavished praise upon this wonderful play, calling Mr. Baitz a major new voice in our theatre. *The Film Society*, set in South Africa, is *not* about the effects of apartheid—at least. overtly. Blenheim is a provincial private school modeled on the second-rate British education machine. It is 1970, a time of complacency for everyone but Terry. a former teacher at Blenheim, who has lost his job because of his connections with Blacks (he invited a Black priest to speak at commencement). Terry tries to involve Jonathan, another teacher at the school and the central character in this play; but Jonathan cares only about his film society, which he wants to keep going at all costs—even if it means programming only safe, non-objectionable, films. When Jonathan's mother, a local rich lady, promises to donate a substantial amount of money to Blenheim if Jonathan is made Headmaster, he must finally choose which side he is on: Terry's or The Establishment's. "Using the school as a microcosm for South Africa, Baitz explores the psychological workings of repression in a society that has to kill its conscience in order to persist in a course of action it knows enough to abhor but cannot afford to relinquish."—New Yorker. "What distinguishes Mr. Baitz' writing, aside from its manifest literacy, is its ability to embrace the ambiguities of political and moral dilemmas that might easily be reduced to blacks and whites."—N.Y. Times. "A beautiful, accomplished play . . . things I thought I was a churl still to value or expect—things like character, plot and theatre dialogue— really do matter."—N.Y. Daily News.   (#8123)

THE SUBSTANCE OF FIRE
Jon Robin Baitz
(Little Theatre.) Drama
3m., 2f. 2 Ints.

Isaac Geldhart, the scion of a family-owned publisher in New York which specializes in scholarly books, suddenly finds himself under siege. His firm is under imminent threat of a corporate takeover, engineered by his own son, Aaron, who watches the bottom line and sees the firm's profitability steadily declining. Aaron wants to publish a trashy novel which will certainly bring in the bucks; whereas Isaac wants to go on publishing worthy scholarly efforts such as his latest project, a multi-volume history of Nazi medical experiments during the Holocaust. Aaron has the bucks to effectively wrench control of the company from his father—or, rather, he has the yen (Japanese businessmen are backing him). What he needs are the votes of the other minority shareholders: his brother Martin and sister Sarah. Like Aaron, they have lived their lives under the thumb of Isaac's imperiousness; and, reluctantly, they agree to side with Aaron against the old man. In the second act, we are back in the library of Isaac's townhouse, a few years later. Isaac has been forcibly retired and has gotten so irascible and eccentric that he may possibly be *non compos mentis*. His children think so, which is why they have asked a psychiatric social worker from the court to interview Isaac to judge his competence. Isaac, who has survived the Holocaust and the death of his wife to build an important publishing company from scratch, must now face his greatest challenge—to persuade Marge Hackett that he is sane. "A deeply compassionate play."—N.Y. Times. "A remarkably intelligent drama. Baitz assimilates and refracts this intellectual history without stinting either on heart or his own original vision."—N.Y. Newsday.   (#21379)

THE NORMAL HEART

(Advanced Groups.) Drama. Larry Kramer. 8m., 1f. Unit set. The New York Shakespeare Festival had quite a success with this searing drama about public and private indifference to the Acquired Immune Deficiency Syndrome plague, commonly called AIDS, and about one man's lonely fight to wake the world up to the crisis. The play has subsequently been produced to great acclaim in London and Los Angeles. Brad Davis originated the role of Ned Weeks, a gay activist enraged at the foot-dragging of both elected public officials and the gay community itself regarding AIDS. Ned not only is trying to save the world from itself, he also must confront the personal toll of AIDS when his lover contracts the disease and ultimately dies. This is more than just a gay play about a gay issue. This is a public health issue which affects all of us. He further uses this theatrical platform to plead with gay brethren to stop thinking of themselves only in terms of their sexuality, and that rampant sexual promiscuity will not only almost guarantee that they will contract AIDS; it is also bad for them as human beings. "An angry, unremitting and gripping piece of political theatre."—N.Y. Daily News. "Like the best social playwright, Kramer produces a cross-fire of life and death energies that illuminate the many issues and create a fierce and moving human drama."—Newsweek. $4.50. (Royalty $60-$40.) Slightly Restricted.   (#788)

A QUIET END

(Adult Groups.) Drama. Robin Swados. 5m. Int. Three men—a schoolteacher, an aspiring jazz pianist and an unemployed actor—have been placed in a run-down Manhattan apartment. All have lost their jobs, all have been shunned by their families, and all have AIDS. They have little in common, it seems, apart from their slowing evolving, albeit uneasy, friendships with each other, and their own mortality. The interaction of the men with a psychiatrist (heard but not seen throughout the course of the play) and the entrance into this arena of the ex-lover of one of the three—seemingly healthy, yet unsure of his future—opens up the play's true concerns: the meaning of friendship, loyalty and love. By celebrating the lives of four men who, in the face of death, become more fearlessly life-embracing instead of choosing the easier path to a quiet end, the play explores the human side of the AIDS crisis, examining how we choose to lead our lives—and how we choose to end them. "The play, as quiet in its message as in its ending, gets the measure of pain and love in a bitter-chill climate."—N.Y. Post. "In a situation that will be recognizable to most gay people, it is the chosen family rather than the biological family, that has become important to these men. Robin Swados has made an impressive debut with A *Quiet End* by accurately representing the touching relationships in such a group."—N.Y. Native. (Royalty $60-$40.) Music Note: Samuel French, Inc. can supply a cassette tape of music from the original New York production, composed by Robin Swados, upon receipt of a refundable deposit of $25.00, (tape must be returned within one week from the close of your production) and a rental fee of $15.00 **per performance.** Use of this music in productions is optional.   (#19017)

SULLIVAN AND GILBERT
(Little Theatre/Musical)
by Ken Ludwig
music by Sir Arthur Sullivan
lyrics by William S. Gilbert

8 male, 4 female, Ints.

Gilbert & Sullivan created some of the world's best-loved musical theatre; but they did not make beautiful music together. Eventually their collaboration ended, riven by Sullivan's chafing at Gilbert's pretensions as a "serious poet" and Gilbert's jealousy over the fact that Sullivan had been knighted and he hadn't. In 1890 Gilbert and Sullivan, who have been at each other's throats for years, are forced to work together one more time: Queen Victoria has requested a command performance of their most popular songs. So, they are putting together a revue of, well--Gilbert & Sullivan's Greatest Hits, complicated by the presence of Arthur, Duke of Edinburgh, son of Queen Victoria, whom Sullivan has agreed to allow to perform in the show, *much* to the consternation of Gilbert, who considers the Duke to be a "dumbbell with a title". Also present is Richard D'Oyly Carte, valiantly trying to mediate, as well as the principal Savoyards of the day, who perform delightfully songs from *The Mikado, Ruddigore,, Iolanthe, Princess Ida, H.M.S. Pinafore, Patience* and *The Pirates of Penzance.* "A charming show."--Boston Globe. Music on rental. #21385

THE NIGHT HANK WILLIAMS DIED
(Little Theatre)
(COMIC/DRAMA)
by Larry L. King

4 male, 2 female, Int.

Thurmond Stottle, once the local high school football hero, is reduced to pumping gas at the local Gulf Station in the tiny West Texas town of Stanley. Thurmond has big dreams, though--he wants to make it as a songwriter and country singer like his hero, the late Hank Williams. He whiles away his free time hanging out in the local bar run by Gus Gilbert, on whom he tries out his latest tunes, and waits for the right moment to take off for Nashville. The moment arrives along with Nellie Bess Powers Clark, his ex-high school sweetheart, who has returned home as her marriage is breaking up. Nellie and Thurmond re-kindle the old flames, and Thurmond plans to leave for Nashville with Nellie--if he can get a stake from Gus. When Gus turns him down, he does a very foolish thing: he robs the gas station, bludgeoning the owner. He returns to Gus' bar to hide and decide what to do; but the sheriff knows just where to find him . . . "A wistful yet mordant folk play. Its theme ...is timeless."--Chr. Sc. Mon. "The plot is strong, and there is no lack of incident or characters, but it is the rich Texas vernacular--the rat-tat-tat of startling, bawdy similes and the funny throwaway lines--that gives the show its texture."--New Yorker. "Amusing and ultimately poignant. A fine, new play "--N.Y. Times. Write for details about music. #15989

LEND ME A TENOR
(Farce)
by KENNETH LUDWIG

4 male, 4 female

This is the biggest night in history of the Cleveland Grand Opera Company, for this night in September, 1934, world-famous tenor Tito Morelli (also known as "Il Stupendo") is to perform his greatest role ("Otello") at the gala season-opening benefit performance which Mr. Saunders, the General Manager, hopes will put Cleveland on the operatic map. Morelli is late in arriving--and when he finally sweeps in, it is too late to rehearse with the company. Through a wonderfully hilarious series of mishaps, Il Stupendo is given a double dose of tranquilizers which, mixed with all the booze he has consumed, causes him to pass out. His pulse is so low that Saunders and his assistant, Max, believe to their horror that he has died. What to do? What to do? Max is an aspiring singer, and Saunders persuades him to black up, get into Morelli's Otello costume, and try to fool the audience into thinking that's Il Stupendo up there. Max succeeds admirably, but the comic sparks really fly when Morelli comes to and gets into his other costume. Now we have *two* Otellos running around, in costume, and two women running around, in lingerie -- each thinking she is with Il Stupendo! A sensation on Broadway and in London's West End. "A jolly play."--NY Times. "Non-stop laughter"--Variety. "Uproarious! Hysterical!"--USA Today. "A rib-tickling comedy."--NY Post. (#667) **Posters.**

POSTMORTEM
(Thriller)
by KENNETH LUDWIG

4 male, 4 female . Int..

Famous actor-manager and playwright William Gillette, best known for over a generation as Sherlock Holmes in his hugely-successful adaptation of Conan Doyle (which is *still* a popular play in the Samuel French Catalogue), has invited the cast of his latest revival of the play up for a weekend at his home in Connecticut, a magnificent pseudo-medieval, Rhenish castle on a bluff overlooking the Connecticut River. Someone is trying to murder William Gillette, and he has reason to suspect that it is one of his guests for the weekend. Perhaps the murderer is the same villain who did away with Gillette's fiancee a year ago if you believe, as does Gillette, that her death was not--as the authorities concluded--a suicide. Gillette's guests include his current ingenue/leading lady and her boyfriend, his Moriarty and his wife, and Gillette's delightfully acerbic sister. For the evening's entertainment Gillette has arranged a seance, conducted by the mysterious Louise Perradine, an actress twenty years before but now a psychic medium. The intrepid and more than slightly eccentric William Gillette has taken on, in "real life", his greatest role: he plans to solve the case *a la* Sherlock Holmes! The seance is wonderfully eerie, revealing one guest's closely-guarded secret and sending another into hysterics, another into a swoon, as Gillette puts all the pieces of the mystery together before the string of attempts on his life leads to a rousingly melodramatic finale. " shots in the dark and darkly held secrets, deathbed letters, guns and knives and bottles bashed over the head, ghosts and hiders behind curtains and misbegotten suspicions. There are moments when you'll jump. Guaranteed."--The Telegraph. (#18677)